KING ALF

D0410708

Languages and Dialects of London School Children

Languages and Dialects of London School Children

An investigation

Harold Rosen and Tony Burgess

Ward Lock Educational

ISBN 0 7062 4087 1

First published 1980

Set in 11 on 12 point Baskerville by Jubal Multiwrite Ltd, London SE13
for Ward Lock Educational
116 Baker Street, W1M 2BB
A member of the Pentos Group
Reproduced from copy supplied
printed and bound in Great Britain
by Billing and Sons Limited
Guildford, London, Oxford, Worcester

Contents

Acknowledgments

Our thanks in the first place to the Centre for Information and Advice on Disadvantage in Education, in particular Colin Roberts and Roger Watkins, for initiating and sustaining discussions between ourselves and the Department of Education and Science, to Eric Bolton HMI for general encouragement and seeing us through problems of time and money. The Inner London Education Authority did everything in its power to ease our path; Peter Newsam, the Chief Education Officer, lent his support; Dr Marten Shipman gave generously of time and expertise; the English Inspectors, John Welch and Geoffrey Thornton made valuable suggestions about the design of the questionnaire and the selection of schools, while Tony Lenney and Mike Egan eased our path into Haringey schools.

None of those we have mentioned will begrudge our acknowledgment of our deepest debt, the one we owe to the teachers in the schools and their pupils who did more than help us unstintingly, even at times providing us with an operations room, beautifully precise special timetables and teams of teachers. They also gave us their insights and inside knowledge. There are, too, all those who have worked with us on our project on language in inner-city schools. They have been consistent members of working parties and of committees, writers of papers and participants in a series of conferences. This publication grows out of their work over several years.

Within the Institute itself we were able to turn to additional resources. Professor Harvey Goldstein and Anne Hawkins of the Department of Statistics kept a watchful and friendly eye from the start on our statistical procedures and Tony Burgess could count on Anne Hawkins to see that our dialogue with the computer would be productive. Teachers on advanced courses in the English Department constituted small teams to assist the schools in collecting data so that schools were assured for at least one day of powerful back-up. Antoinette Pernetta, our secretary, sustained us all throughout and Shyama Iyer with a vigilant eye typed and discreetly edited the final version.

The writing up of the report grew from planning and discussion by Harold Rosen, Tony Burgess, Jane Miller and John Snodgrass. Harold Rosen wrote Chapters 1, 2 and 4 and Tony Burgess Chapter 3. In addition to their general contribution John Snodgrass contributed material on bilingualism and Jane Miller on examinations and the study of linguistic diversity in school.

Tony Burgess was seconded from the English Department to act as Research Officer and carried the weight of the work of devising the questionnaire, piloting it through two schools, organizing the survey and analysing the figures. The report rests on his major contribution.

Harold Rosen

Chapter 1   Introduction

In September 1977, through the good offices of the Centre for Educational Disadvantage, we received a small grant from the Department of Education and Science to enable us to carry out a limited survey of linguistic diversity in inner-London schools. The scale of the operation can best be judged by the fact that it made possible in the first instance the employment of one research officer and a half-time secretary for six months. It was later generously extended by four months. Nine months after the granting of the research fund, an interim report, based on the results in eighteen schools was submitted to the DES. This, our second and full account, is based on the results from twenty-eight schools.

Thus the conditions unavoidably imposed on the survey meant that it had to be carried out within a very short period with very slender resources. Indeed, without the assistance of advanced students (all experienced teachers) of the English Department at the University of London Institute of Education, it would have been a circumscribed and perfunctory operation. We mention these constraints not by way of apology but simply to set the record straight and to claim no more for our study than it merits. On the other hand, it gives us no little satisfaction to record that, as far as we know, our investigation is the first of its kind to be carried out in the United Kingdom, and it constitutes a pioneer study. We are confident its findings will arouse widespread serious interest and lead to further and broader investigation which will disperse national and local ignorance. We are the more optimistic on this score since there are already moves afoot to replicate our survey in other areas.

Anyone could be forgiven for believing that the information we were seeking was simple and straightforward and therefore to be obtained speedily and easily and that a questionnaire consisting of a handful of questions would suffice. Indeed we know of such attempts and sympathise with them. A hard-

1

pressed authority or school must do what it can, often without time for preparation. Anxieties about one particular minority or another have led to enquiries relating to that and nothing else. Information acquired in this way is useful but circumscribed. It can tell us about greater numbers of pupils but much less about them. Moreover, it tends to make data-gathering just that and nothing more rather than one part of a process which draws on the researchers, teachers and pupils who learn as they go on what linguistic diversity means.

This kind of information is not to be had for the mere asking, nor can school records be milked for it. What languages and dialects people speak is for them a delicate personal, social, and at times, political matter. There are compelling resons for being reluctant to speak about such matters and the information is dauntingly complex. We explain this more fully in our next chapter; at this point let us emphasize that no nice sharp dividing lines separate many of our categories. When do you say that for practical purposes someone is no longer speaking like a foreigner? When we say, 'She can also speak Turkish', what does that mean? If you recognize someone as a Yorkshire speaker, does he speak a Yorkshire dialect? Clearly some relatively refined judgments are called for and certain conceptual problems grappled with. For these reasons, in the following pages we have to consider what we mean by languages, dialects and creoles, we have to distinguish between variations in the speech of an individual and variations in a community of speakers, and we have to consider some of the different ways in which school pupils know a second language. There are many children now who grow up able to understand a language quite well but speak it very little and read and write it not at all. These and other considerations led us to devote as much care to the construction of our questionnaire (see Appendix 2) as we dared in the short time available. We explain the thinking behind it elsewhere (see Chapter 3). It was our hope that with refinements and modifications its life would extend beyond our short study.

It was our ambitious assumption that, in addition to those data-gatherers we could put in the field, teachers in their schools would carry the main burden of the enquiry. This in its turn had its own consequences:

(i) The questionnaire needed to be a compromise between

the delicacy of information we would have liked to obtain and what it would be reasonable to expect to collect with the assistance of teachers who made no special claim to expert knowledge. (As it turned out they were often unduly modest.)

(ii) We needed to make a firm commitment to schools to conduct at least one briefing session before the survey work began, to offer help at peak-periods of data-collection in the schools, and to offer, as far as we were competent to do so, to resolve difficult cases.

(iii) The questionnaire needed to be prefaced by an intro-duction (see Appendix 1) which would act as a lucid guide for teachers without obliging them to undertake a major intellectual chore.

We were determined that, slender though our resources were, we would offer a support system to schools which would transform the operation from a perfunctory form-filling one to an active collaborative one. As we saw it, the survey would not simply provide valuable new information but also serve as an instrument of in-service education sensitizing teachers to the configuration of diversity, improving their knowledge of their own pupils' language and setting in train a reconsideration of policies and practices. For our own part only our active participation and encounters with pupils could have deepened our own understanding and knowledge. We have listened to the speakers who end up in our statistical tables, we have listened to pupils talking about their language and we have joined with many teachers in discussing the educational meaning of what we have heard.

Our previous work in inner-city schools persuaded us that we should be concerned with the language of all pupils. This was not because of some vague democratic sentiment. We believe teachers confront language diversity in that way in their daily teaching. Their concern is how to work with pupils of all kinds. To be sure, particular groups merit attention for particular purposes (learning English, for instance). But linguistic diver-sity as a phenomenon has always been present in our schools. There is scarcely an issue raised by the richer diversity of languages and dialects which was not there before. In one way or another we have been concerned for a century with the interaction of the experience, culture and language which pupils bring to school. The issues are not new ones but they are in the new context much harder to ignore. So it was not our view that our sole concern was with ethnic-cultural minorities of recent immigrations. A central and novel feature of our survey was that it *aimed at covering the whole pattern of diversity, a pattern to which the language of every pupil would contribute.* We also took the view that linguistic diversity is potentially a source of strength, an access of new resources and new abilities. With the help of teachers, we were thus able to present our survey in a very positive way, as a roll-call of language resources rather than an interrogation. Pupils could be encouraged to take pride in the languages and dialects they could muster and an interest in the nature of language variety.

In sum, we wanted the survey to be as much of a joint enterprise as possible involving cooperation amongst researchers, teachers and pupils and acting as part of an educative process in the context of a multi-cultural society. It followed that the investigation was above all a school-by-school operation, a slow but rewarding procedure.

A questionnaire remains a questionnaire. We do not deceive ourselves that the information we have gathered is exhaustive nor that it is always as precise as ideal conditions might have made it. Only a huge team of experts with rich resources and plenty of time could even begin to make that claim. Both the teachers and researchers came upon valuable information which could not be incorporated within the framework of the questionnaire. At times we lacked the expertise or the 'ear' to make discriminations which we knew to exist (e.g. between different Caribbean dialects) and had to rely on oblique sources like biographical facts. There must have been occasions when, through shyness or other kinds of reluctance, we failed to elicit information. Basically the data are derived from teachers' existing knowledge, often very expert in certain areas, and talk with pupils, usually in small groups. We remain certain that the quality of our information is good and that we were right to strike out beyond the barest basic responses. At the same time, enough work has been done in sociolinguistics to show how subtle and complex are the phenomena of bilingualism and bidialectalism: only case studies can do justice to the living language of our school pupils.

Such were the circumstances and our intentions. It was a reasonable corollary that this report should be much more than a bald presentation of statistics and interpretative comment. We want it to serve as a basis for discussion of the most important issues surrounding the data. We have, therefore, placed the figures and their immediate meaning in a context which attempts to elucidate in a non-technical manner the current thinking about languages, dialects, bilingualism etc. and to relate it to the London setting. We go on to show how a survey, as we conceived it, actually takes place. Then, after discussing the figures, we go on to suggest what the educational implications of our findings might be. That final section points to the future. It is part of the agenda for a multi-cultural society. It takes us well beyond tables and percentages. We, and those associated with us in this survey, have begun to work on that agenda and feel better equipped by virtue of the experience reported in these pages.

Chapter 2   Linguistic diversity

1   WHY STUDY LINGUISTIC DIVERSITY IN SCHOOLS?

Language teaching in our schools has for a long time been of two distinct kinds. On the one hand there has been the teaching of English, the 'national' language, the mother tongue, as we say, and on the other, the teaching of a few privileged (European) foreign languages, modern and classical. Both kinds of teaching have traditionally included a strong component of literary study. These relatively calm curriculum waters have until recently been unruffled by serious challenges to their powerful rights to their curriculum space, or by recognition that their scope and clienteles had undergone radical change.

We came to this investigation by a route which we wish to map out because it will explain why we chose to adopt one procedure rather than another and perhaps it will account for certain biases in our discussion. It may also come as something of a surprise that a department of the University of London Institute of Education, the central concern of which is the teaching of English as a mother tongue, undertook such a task. The basic assumption, so basic as never to have been questioned, behind the teaching of English in our schools, was that English is the mother tongue of our pupils and that the task of the teacher was to make pupils literate in that mother tongue and to extend their use of it in ways which the spontaneous energies of the community could not ensure.

Anyone who knows our schools also knows that the basic assumption can no longer be seriously sustained. It was always a convenient fiction. There were always children who were Welsh and Gaelic speakers, there were speakers of regional dialects and small groups of immigrant pupils speaking a variety of languages. But such were the numbers involved and such were the political and social circumstances that these facts could be regarded as marginal. If language variety was a matter of significant concern

Prior to mass immigrat

6

it tended to be focused on differences of attainment or supposed differences of potential or problems believed to derive from vernacular speech.

All that has changed dramatically. In the space of twenty years the configuration of linguistic diversity in the schools has been altered beyond recognition. Our school population contains large numbers of pupils for whom English is a second, perhaps third, language; there are also pupils who are fluent speakers of English but who also speak another language; there are speakers who have in their repertoire an overseas dialect of English or a British-based form of it.

How could this be a matter of concern for teachers of English as a mother tongue? Many of us when we first encountered this new diversity resolved all questions in a simple and, as it seemed to us then, in a credible fashion. Those children who could not speak English or who were still beyond doubt in the early stages of learning it were somebody else's business. The English-as-a-second-language teachers would give them sufficient mastery of English to equip them to enter the English-as-a-mother tongue classroom. Once there, they would be essentially no different from other pupils in the classroom. Business as usual. As for those boys and girls speaking a dialect of English which we found difficult to understand, like a Caribbean creole, perhaps they too should undergo some special treatment which would convert them into speakers of British English? In any case, given enough time, they would soon pick up the habits of the natives. They would be no better or worse than their fellow-pupils, speakers of a variety of London English or Birmingham English or Bradford English.

Looking back on those early days we can easily see now how sanguine we were, though there were, of course, honourable exceptions. As Perren (1979) has pointed out, the sole concern was with teaching English. Little or no interest was taken in the language and dialects they already possessed. As Verity Khan very sharply puts it, writing as late as 1978:

The first perspective is that of the mainstream school, which in Britain remains monocultural and monolingual. It does not recognize or accord value to the culture and language of children of minorities ... Schools still reflect the two attitudes prevailing in the wider society. Minorities

7

should 'integrate' into the majority society with minimal interference to the *status quo* and 'the sooner the better' despite the likelihood of initial shock and disorientation.

That criticism might well be applied to the 'mainstream school' but, it might be argued, could scarcely be reasonably used as a stick with which to beat the mother tongue teachers of English. They were not equipped, nor could they reasonably be expected to be equipped, with a knowledge of the dozens of languages with which they are now confronted; much less could they be expected to improvise strategies, materials and the kind of teaching now required of schools. With some justification they could declare it was not their business.

However, an inexorable educational logic obliged more and more of them (ourselves included) to abandon this position. Firstly the stubborn reality of classrooms showed teachers that they must expect to be teaching pupils who could not by any stretch of the imagination be equated with pupils for whom British English was a mother tongue. Those who had completed special English second-language learning of one kind or another would almost certainly still be in the process of achieving native-like mastery. Many teachers found that quite frequently pupils would arrive in their classes who spoke not a word of English and whose languages they could in many cases not even identify. But, more creditable than sheer grim necessity which brought about the first important shifts in attitude, many teachers of English were committed to the principle that the language pupils bring to school was much more than a narrowly linguistic possession: it was rather the medium through which they articulated their most significant experiences and feelings. These teachers were also likely to have an interest in language which went beyond an interest in English. The new diversity of language and dialects, though it might present them with knotty difficulties, was also intellectually and educationally stimulating. Teachers who had begun to explore some of the potentiality of the regional vernaculars of Britain would see a natural extension of this commitment in equipping themselves with a knowledge of Caribbean dialects and deeper under-standing of many other languages.

More and more pupils in schools who were born and bred in this country, for whom English in some sense was a first language, continued to have in their repertoires an overseas dialect or

8

another language. Was this of no concern to the English mother tongue teacher? Should he not know the nature of the pupil's linguistic allegiances? Teachers of English were also becoming drawn into the rapidly developing work on language across the curriculum and clearly they needed to make major adjustments in their thinking to accommodate new kinds of needs.

Gradually many of us have to come to realize that the diversity of language in our schools must be seen in a much wider context. We are talking in fact about what we now call multicultural education. The Bullock Report (HMSO, 1975) which attempted a comprehensive purview of language in education pointed us in this direction.

It is clear from available reports that comparatively little provision is made in some areas, that the education of children of overseas parentage is given low priority, and that many of the existing arrangements do little more than meet the initial language and adjustment needs of new arrivals. It is, of course, at that point that the need for intervention is most sharply felt in the schools, but the adjustment of immigrant children to their new environment and to learning elementary English is only the beginning of what for most is a long process. It is a process that consists primarily of learning to live in or between two cultures, and of learning to handle two languages or dialects. (20.2 p.284)

The passage is inevitably somewhat dated and does not envisage the novel cultural experience which emerges from the diversity: but it does ask us to go deeper than language and it also warns that the issues raised will not go away, they are, the Report continues, of a 'long term nature'. The boldest statement in whole Report is perhaps,

No child should be expected to cast off the language and culture of the home as he crosses the school threshold, nor to live and act as though school and home represent two totally separate and different cultures which have to be kept firmly apart. (20.5 p.286)

It is heartening to see in this statement, which appears in the

9

context of a discussion of reading and language difficulties of 'children from families of overseas origin', a principle asserted which is of universal application: the telling phrase is 'no child'. All teachers need to work out the implications but perhaps no one more than the mother tongue teachers of English. In the end, all pupils arrive in their classrooms, so that they are obliged to concern themselves not so much with the needs of special sub-groups but with how all the pupils with all their diversity will interact and how they should change their teaching to ensure that this interaction will be positive, enriching and educative. To do this means knowing as much as possible about linguistic diversity rather than ignoring it.

We have begun with this discussion to show how it came about that we found ourselves exploring relatively unfamiliar terrain and making ourselves much more familiar with aspects of language and languages which had hitherto been at best at the periphery of our preoccupations. Whatever deficiencies there may have been in our personal equipment for carrying out our task, we started with some advantages. We were seeing language diversity as a whole. Valuable work has been done and is being done which takes as its focus this linguistic group or that. Mostly it has been concerned with bilingualism. (See for example Lewis, 1970; Sharp *et al*, 1973; Sharp, 1973.)

The conference called by the Centre for Information on Language Teaching and Research, and reported in *Bilingualism and British Education: the Dimensions of Diversity* (CILT, 1976) reveals something of the emphasis of most current work and its imbalance. Two papers deal with linguistic minorities and provision for language maintenance, five papers with bilingualism, three of which are devoted to the situation in Wales and one on foreign language teaching. By contrast we are disposed to look at diversity from the other side. Beams of light have been focused on particular groups; we wanted a more general illumination which would be of value to whole schools and to those who needed to consider policy for all children at any level.

Up to this point we have tried to give a general explanation of our involvement and to show how we shared with teachers of English a certain history. Our recent work took us much more directly towards our latest study. For several years our research work has been centred on language in inner-city schools and through conferences and working parties we have worked closely with teacher colleagues who wished to join with us in an attempt to define the issues and look afresh at problems of teaching and learning language in the inner-city setting. By this means we built up a considerable communication network, and we were able to assemble a collective understanding of language in London schools. Inevitably discussions and studies returned repeatedly to the theme of language diversity. It soon became clear to us that individually and collectively none of us possessed really hard information about the languages and dialects spoken by the school population. At that stage it made sense to produce a do-it-yourself instrument to enable teachers to carry out their own small-scale investigations. In February 1977 we produced *Guidelines for the Investigation of the Language of Inner-city Pupils* (Institute of Education, 1977). The lineaments of the questionnaire (See Appendix 2) produced for the investigation reported here can be traced in that earlier document. This applies not only to the questions to which we were trying to obtain answers but also to the way in which we saw teachers and pupils as active participants in the process of obtaining them. In ambition it went far beyond anything which could be used in a wider-scale short-term investigation. It assumed a *sustained* interest on the part of the teachers in one school and a shared exploration with pupils. One extract will suffice to illustrate its scope and to underline the ways in which the results we report in these pages can only be a prelude to a deeper and more refined study.

2.1. **A language other than English**

2.1.1 If your pupil's mother tongue is a language other than English, say which language.

2.1.2. Where exactly is the pupil's form of this language spoken outside Britain?

2.1.3. Do you know anything of the 'status' of this language both here and in its country of origin?
(a) How is it regarded by speakers of it?
(b) How is it regarded by others?
(Note: We think this question may well prove difficult. But you might be able to find out such things as whether the language is thought of as 'sub-standard', the language of an elite, etc. Do what you can.)

2.1.4. Is literacy well established in the language?

2.1.5. Is there an indigenous literature (in the narrow sense) in the language. Oral? Written?

11

2.1.6.   Are there special aspects of this language which should be noted, e.g. the existence of geographical and/or social differences as in Greek demotic and Katharevousa.

2.1.7.   Are printed materials available in this country? Can you specify (newspapers, magazines, books).

2.1.8.   Are films in this language accessible to the pupil?

2.1.9.   To what extent is there an awareness among the teaching staff about this pupil's language.

2.1.10.   Is the pupil literate in this language? If the answer is yes, give a rough-and-ready estimate of his/her level (A, B, C).

2.1.11.   For what purposes, if any, does the pupil use this language
     — at home?
     — in the neighbourhood in general (shops, clubs etc.)?
     — in the neighbourhood — peer group?
     — for talking to the older generation?
     — religion?

2.1.12.   Does the pupil have access to teaching in this language?
     Does the pupil have access to teaching of this language?

2.1.13.   If the answer to either of these questions is yes, give as many details as you can including whether it is in or out of your school.

2.1.14.   Did the pupil receive teaching in and/or of this language in some form of schooling, before coming to this country.
     Details.

2.1.15.   Describe where and how this pupil has learnt and is learning English?

2.1.16.   What variety of spoken English does the pupil use? (Predominantly the recognizable speech of a foreigner, predominantly a London or other region dialect, predominantly Received Pronunciation.)

2.1.17.   Give some indication of the pupil's competence as a speaker of English. If you wish you could use these categories (a) beginner, (b) transitional, (c) very like a native speaker.

2.1.18.   To what extent is his level of competence reflected in his reading and writing in English.

2.1.19.   If this pupil has some competence in another non-English language or languages, describe briefly his

relationship to it along the lines of the above questions.
As a teacher do you find it useful to know this?

Events overtook us. Later in the year we were given a grant
to carry out our present study and had to give our full attention
to it. What we had been able to do was to think through some
of the complexities of linguistic diversity and the range of
information and knowledge we were seeking. It was, then,
through our work in trying 'to take the first steps towards
building a picture of the language situation in inner-city schools'
(as we said in the *Guidelines*) that we eventually found ourselves immersed in our investigation, and chose our ways of
reaching the declared goal which were different from readily
available alternatives.

2   INVESTIGATING LINGUISTIC DIVERSITY

The community of linguistic scholars in this country has shown
remarkably little interest in the new linguistic profile which has
emerged in the last twenty years. We have scholars who can tell
us more about linguistic diversity in remote African and Asian
communities than they can about the diversity under their
noses. That is perhaps not to be wondered at. The monolingual
tradition dies hard and for a long time it made superficial
sense to regard Britain as more unified linguistically than any
other major industrial country, certainly more than France,
Germany, Italy or the United States (see Stephens, 1976).
The study of diversity has been concentrated on regional and
social dialects (Orton *et al*, 1974 and Trudgill, 1978) and has
had a strong historical bias (Lockwood, 1975). Orton's monu-
mental work was essentially an historical salvage operation
attempting to record and map dialect diversity before it dis-
appeared from its rural strongholds. Trudgill and his collaborators
have used sociolinguistic sophistication to reveal what is alive
and changing in current vernacular English. It is of particular
interest to us since it encompasses urban dialects.

Bilingualism is seen through the Welsh and Gaelic experiences.
These emphases, helpful in their own ways, have not provided
us with a picture of contemporary diversity and an understanding of the new linguistic minorities which have grown up
in the very recent past. It was only to be expected that those

13

whose interests were in societies where a multiplicity of languages coexisted and interacted would look to such countries as India, Central America and Africa, but the social and cultural circumstances of those countries are so different from our own as to make the work only minimally relevant. (See, for example, Parkin, 1977, who shows how multilingualism in urban Kenya has its specific features.) They have, moreover, generally been motivated by a linguistic interest in languages about which little or nothing was known. Nevertheless, some of the literature raises matters of general principle which are highly relevant to our very specific study. Stewart (1968) proposed the development of a 'framework for describing national multilingualism' which would 'emphasize social, functional and distributional relationships within (and to some extent across) national boundaries'. When we produce figures for, let us say, the number of speakers for Gujerati, these tell us nothing about the status of that language in its country of origin nor about how the critical social description may have changed over a period within a speech community in this country. We shall return to this question in our final discussion.

Attempts have been made to produce a condensed algebraic formula which would present a sociolinguistic profile for a given population (Greenberg, 1956; Lieberson, 1964; Ferguson, 1966). This approach seems promising for providing a statistical shorthand for representing the results of surveys. It might well come into its own when we have a number of studies similar to our own, for its value lies essentially in the provision of a *comparative* index. We must also remind ourselves just how unreliable most national statistics are since they base themselves on such things as the census, deducing from ethnic allegiances and other extrapolations. There is almost no published guidance on the conduct of language surveys. The exception is Ohannessian *et al, Language Surveys in Developing Nations* (1975). This, as its title suggests, is relevant to contexts very different from Britain and gives details for methods and techniques suitable for large teams working over a long period. However, it contains a questionnaire for use in Ghana (p.172) which is a model of its kind and could well be adapted for use in this country by teams of that sort.

The languages spoken by London school pupils will in many cases be related to 'ethnicity'. As Fishman (1977) has argued, language can often be the most salient symbol of ethnicity because it carries the past and expresses the present and future attitudes and aspirations. Giles (1977) has collected together very new work in this field and, linking social psychology and linguistics, explored linguistic diversity from the perspective of inter-group relations when the groups have distinct ethnic identities. School is one of those domains where sustained relations of this kind occur. We still need to know how far the possession of a language (or even an accent; see Bourhis and Giles, 1977) by a pupil is in fact also a symbol of ethnicity, but first of all we need to know that he possesses it. But there is no simple relationship between ethnicity and language especially in multilinguistic communities.

Many contemporary communities consist of people drawn recently and rapidly from distant ethnic groups as a result of extensive colonial administration, labour migration, industrial urbanization and political statehood. Within such polyethnic communities, diversity of speech rather than of flora and fauna provides the most readily available 'raw' classificatory data for the differentiation of new social groups and the redefinition of old ones. (Parkin, op.cit.)

We were concerned with a specific school population in inner-London schools since we are convinced that from an educational viewpoint what matters in the end is what happens at school level. A linguistic minority which might be considered to be so insignificant at national level as to be ignored, becomes hugely significant if its children constitute a high proportion of the pupils of one school. It was a relatively intimate picture we were after. Moreover, it was soon evident to us that we could derive little comfort or illumination from other sets of statistics. For a country as highly organized as ours and with sophisticated data-collection resources, it is startling and even shocking that the blunt truth is that at national level we can only provide rough guesses, at local authority level we are even more in the dark (with a few exceptions) and at school level there are only isolated instances of schools which have hard figures on their populations. Of course, we have been bedevilled by the political controversy which has surrounded minority groups and there has been a justifiable fear that statistics relating to minority groups might become political missiles. It remains a

15

lamentable fact that all those, and there are many, who have been anxious to reconsider curricula in the light of the cultural, social and linguistic composition of schools have had to work with only sketchy information.

3   LINGUISTIC DIVERSITY IN BRITAIN

How limited is our knowledge is best illustrated by our dependence on the 1971 census. A recent analysis of these figures by Campbell-Platt (1976) is preceded by the gloomy comment that, 'It is impossible to construct, from published sources, an accurate linguistic map of minorities in Britain'. This was echoed and amplified by Derrick (1977):

> Not only do we know very little about how our immigrants see themselves and their future, but we know very little too about their attitudes to their mother tongues. It would seem reasonable for local authorities to want to know more about potential mother-tongue language-learners themselves before embarking on any large-scale new policy, especially, one might add, when there are still unresolved difficulties about the policy of teaching English as a second language in schools.
>
> What emerges most clearly from the CILT conference report [i.e. CILT 1976, ed] is how little is known about language and minority groups in Britain and what a need there is for reliable information if any far reaching decisions about the curriculum are to be made. In the first place we do not have any accurate information about what vernaculars are spoken by minority groups, by what numbers and to what extent. The kind of sociolinguistic information that went into Fishman's work in America does not yet exist in Britain.

It might be added wryly that the dearth of study and information applies not only to minority groups but to vernacular speakers of all kinds in Britain with the exception of the Welsh and Gaelic-speaking Scots. In Bradford and Bedford where special projects are afoot there is considerably more detailed information available to the educational authorities.

Although we cannot offer anything like the studies which

abound in Canada and the United States, there are signs that sustained attention will be given in the future to the languages and dialects in Britain. Khan's paper for the Runnymede Trust (1978) on linguistic minorities is now to be followed by a major piece of research under her directorship, the *Linguistic Minorities Project,** in which a multi-disciplinary team of researchers will aim at providing an account and analysis of changing patterns of bilingualism in a representative selection of areas of England. The research will include a sociolinguistic survey and a more detailed study of patterns of language use and language attitudes.

Trudgill is fostering work on dialects and has made available specialist studies to a wider public. In *Sociolinguistic Patterns of British English* (1979) there is work on urban dialectology, loyalty to vernacular cultures, the grammar of working-class English in Reading, West Yorkshire, Edinburgh, Cheshire and Glasgow, the phonology of Scouse (Liverpool), intonation in Tyneside, change and variation in Belfast English and other detailed studies. His own work on language and social class in Norwich (1974) and on dialect in education (1975 and 1979) has established a rational basis for the discussion of issues which generate heat very easily. Wells (1973), Edwards (1979) and Sutcliffe (forthcoming) have begun what must in due course become a comprehensive study of West Indian English in Britain.

It is to work of this kind that a full sociolinguistic study of language diversity will have to turn. It will be noted how very recent some of it is. It was too recent, in fact, to have helped us in our work.

Since our survey had a statistical core we needed to know what data already existed. Some few local authorities keep careful statistics but they are the exceptions and even at school level there are only isolated instances of schools which have figures. Where data are collected they usually relate to recent immigrations and usually arise from educational and social anxieties often about particular populations. Minorities which have made themselves 'invisible' in the educational system are assumed to raise no cultural/educational issues. If the English of the pupils has a native-like fluency, they cease to be a focus of concern. Native speakers of a variety of British English have

*Housed in the EFL Department of the University of London Institute of Education. Professor H. G. Widdowson is the Chairman of the project.

aroused very little attention in current discussion. Why, for example, have we been so blind to the cultural and linguistic differences of the Irish? In 1851 there were 519,959 Irish born people (5.8% of the total population) in England and Wales. By 1971 there were 709,235 (1.4%). They remain the largest single overseas born group. Between 1881 and 1905 the firmly established but small Jewish community was swollen by a huge emigration from the Tsarist Empire. Almost all were bi- or plurilingual. They spoke Yiddish, were literate in classical Hebrew and usually spoke an East-European language. This group was further increased by refugees from Germany and German-occupied Europe. In the immediate post-war years there were 457,000 migrants from Europe, the largest single group being Poles who numbered 130,000. Some minority groups which have grown rapidly in post-war years were extensions of earlier immigrations and this is often forgotten. The Cypriots, for example, numbered approximately 8,000 in London alone in 1939 and by 1964 the London Cypriot population had grown to 75,000. Italians and those of Italian parentage numbered 20,000 before the Second World War and 140,000 by 1972. These facts serve as a reminder that immigration is not essentially a new experience for Britain nor has it been confined to minorities like the Huguenots who have found themselves a place in history textbooks. Perhaps we should also remember that in Wales the large immigrant population is mostly English!

There seems to be general agreement that the chief linguistic minorities whose origin is, in the main, recent immigration are, in order of numerical strength: Punjabi, Urdu, Bengali, Gujerati, German, Polish, Italian, Greek, Spanish, Cantonese and Hakka. The difficulty is that this view is based largely on the 1971 census which gave figures only for the overseas-born population and that, of course, by country of origin. It would not tell us, for example, whether a Pakistani-born resident spoke Bengali or Urdu or another language, or a Nigerian-born resident spoke Yoruba, Ibo, Hausa or English. Nevertheless, it is relevant to our study to note that the largest overseas-born populations were resident in the Greater London area. Always cosmopolitan in its central areas, London is now a multi-cultural conurbation with minority communities firmly established in the suburbs. Campbell-Platt (*op.cit.*) discusses the probable language distribution of the overseas-born and we give a tabulation below based on her outline.

Countries	Languages
India	Punjabi (50%), Gujerati, Hindi, Bengali, Tamil
Pakistan	Punjabi/Urdu (majority), Bengali
Bangladesh	Bengali
Sri Lanka	Sinhala, Tamil
Cyprus	Greek (majority), Turkish
Hong Kong	Cantonese
African countries	Swahili (as a lingua franca); (Asians) Punjabi, Hindi, Gujerati.

This cannot claim to be more than the crudest of pictures. It does not, of course, tell us anything about bilingualism and plurilingualism and many languages do not figure at all, e.g. Portuguese, Italian, etc.

The census, for all its shortcomings as a reliable source of linguistic data, does give us a breakdown by selected boroughs. We have abstracted from these the figures for Great Britain, the Greater London Council's area, and the Greater London Borough of Haringey to which we gave special attention in our investigation (see Table 1). The figures need to be reinterpreted for the school population to allow for such facts as that the German-origin population is largely from an older pre-war immigration, that they do not include the now numerous British-born members of minority groups and that new groups (e.g. Portuguese) have arrived since 1971. A country of birth criterion also fails to give us the slightest idea of the degree of linguistic assimilation. For how many children is English now a first language? How many can also speak another?

By 1971 more than half the population of West Indian origin was born in Britain. Edwards (1979) while warning that the figure is an estimate suggests that the West Indian population in 1971 was 543,000. Well over half are of Jamaican origin.

Minorities are highly concentrated in the great conurbations and within those conurbations in particular districts. The 1971 census shows that of a total population of New Commonwealth born persons of 1,157,170 (2.1%) Greater London's share was 476,535 (6.4%) to which we can add the Greater Metropolitan area with 106,290 (2.0%). London is then the chief host area

Table 1

	Germany	Italy	Poland	Spain	Malta	Ghana	Kenya	Nigeria	Tanzania
Great Britain	157,680	108,980	110,925	49,470	33,840	11,215	59,500	28,565	14,375
GLC	34,300	32,545	32,505	25,640	8,305	6,840	24,535	18,540	5,905
Haringey	—	1,820	1,190	—	—	—	920	1,290	—

	Uganda	Ceylon	Cyprus	Hong Kong	China	India	Malaysia	Pakistan	Singapore
Great Britain	12,590	17,040	73,295	29,520	13,495	321,995	25,685	139,935	27,335
GLC	5,560	8,470	53,095	6,865	3,815	106,380	8,520	30,135	4,460
Haringey	—	—	11,865	—	—	3,255	—	—	—

Population of GB 53,978,540
Overseas-born 3,088,110

Census 1971

and as an indication of more local concentration we may take
some selected figures of live births for January 1979.

Table 2   Live births to mothers born overseas, January 1979

65%	over 50%	over 40%
Brent	Haringey Kensington	Hammersmith, Newham, Camden, Islington, Lambeth, Wandsworth

4   THE DIMENSIONS OF DIVERSITY

The linguistic literature is rich with studies of language variety
— how one person's language may change in different ways and
in different settings and to fulfil different functions. We have
been shown how each individual's language is as unique as his
fingerprint, how one speech community differs from another in
language, dialect or style. There are differences based on class,
sex, age and ethnicity. To anyone with even a passing interest
in language these differences are fascinating in their richness,
evidence of the inexhaustible inventiveness of mankind. This
is no place to explore all these differences. We shall limit ourselves to those most relevant to our study. Our purpose is
quite simple: it is our hope that this work will be read first
and foremost by teachers, many of whom will have had no
special reasons to delve into the linguistic literature. We wanted
to supply them with the necessary minimum of background to
enable them to read the rest of the work in an informed way.
If we oversimplify for the more informed reader, we are prepared
to take that risk.

We were concerned with London school pupils, youngsters
growing up in a metropolis who cannot be said to belong to a
speech community as that term has often been understood, a
homogeneous linguistic society. Halliday (1978) points out:

A city is not a speech community in the classical sense.
Its inhabitants obviously do not all talk to each other.
They do not speak alike; and furthermore they do not all
mean alike. But a city is an environment in which meanings

21

are exchanged. In this process conflicts arise, symbolic conflicts which are no less real than conflicts over economic interest; and these conflicts contain the mechanism of change ... The city dweller's picture of the universe is not, in the typical instance, one of order and constancy. But at least it has — or could have, if allowed to — a compensating quality that is of some significance: the fact that many very different groups of people have contributed to the making of it.

The 'classical sense' which saw a speech community in simple terms probably never applied, but in London only a most ingenious model could incorporate the distribution of dialects and languages and their interaction: both a geographical model and social class model would be insufficient, although each would contribute. Cockney slips across class boundaries. In London schools there are speakers of Standard who live and learn side by side with all kinds of other speakers. London Black English (which as yet has no accepted name) will be found *par excellence* in Brixton where it is community-based but it might also crop up anywhere else.

Halliday emphasizes the conflicts which arise when 'meanings are exchanged' but it is also true that at any time we can find remarkable examples of people transcending linguistic barriers. It has often been remarked that where the intention to cooperate is paramount, difficulties are overcome which otherwise seem insuperable. They remain difficulties all the same. Fishman's (1965) question applied to London remains to be answered, 'Who speaks what language to whom and when?' We shall go on answering it for a long time before we begin to exhaust the possibilities. By then the situation will have changed!

Change is in fact what is typical of London diversity now. New languages appear, settled languages change as the language X as spoken in X-land becomes the language X as spoken in Britain. (There are well-known precedents here like Pennsylvania Dutch, Norwegian-American.) The Caribbean dialects change into a London variety. Dialects and languages begin to influence each other. Urbanization is a great destroyer of sharply defined frontiers. This does not mean that London is a linguistic melting pot but rather that it is a great transformer of the languages and dialects which arrive on its doorstep. The communication system of a metropolis is so highly developed that very few remain uninfluenced by languages other than their mother tongue. Typically these would be the oldest members of certain immigrant communities, especially women who can remain sealed off, immured within their own speech community.'The more general process at work is the creation of thousands of bilingual and bidialectal speakers whose families were mono-lingual a generation or so back. Which dialect of English they learn depends in the main on their social class position in this country. It is common practice to talk of the 'target language' of a second-language learner. In London it will be a moving target, though undoubtedly most, by virtue of their social position will, consciously or not, have as their model London working-class speech. In school, where the acquisition of Standard is usually seen as an unquestionable goal, this creates additional complexities for the learner.

We shall now give separate consideration to the main dimensions of diversity: (1) the diversity of languages, (2) the diversity of dialects, (3) bilingualism. We shall try to limit our discussion to those themes which shed some light on our figures, on our procedures and on our final discussion.

5   DIVERSITY OF LANGUAGES

The pessimists have never forgotten the Tower of Babel and contemplate the thousands of languages in the world with horror. The rest of us learn to live with it, for the most part nestling in our own language and making a few scurrying sorties into alien territories. A few enjoy it. Optimistically we believe that many more, certainly more teachers, find their new experience of speakers of many languages invigorating.

For certain purposes, it is valuable and constructive to stress what all languages share: that they are an essential and central part of human social life, that the activities we call speaking are indeed amazingly similar, that, as has been repeatedly stressed, no one language is in a privileged position in a league table of worthiness, cognitive potential or grammaticality. For other purposes, however, we do need to be intensely aware that, although languages may be equal, they are also different in significant respects. In our survey the familiar names crop up: Greek, Punjabi, Swahili etc. There are also some much less familiar ones like French Creole, Pushtu, Efic. It must be apparent that the names tell us very little more than the names of countries would in a gazetteer.

Without adopting a determinist stance (the so-called 'Whorf hypothesis', that a given language shapes in a specific way the thought of its speakers) we can say that every language is as it is because it carries within it the imprint of the societies which use it. It therefore matters to teachers that they should know something of this. Further we must come to terms with the fact that the languages we encounter in London start by being uprooted and, as they send down new roots in new communities, undergo change. We may easily say that a child speaks Italian. What does that mean? Tosi (1979) reports that Italians in Bedford do not speak Standard Italian and do not understand it but speak southern regional dialect. The children may speak a second or third generation form of it which is not acceptable in the villages they return to on holiday.

A language may be spoken by a small number of people in a compact community within a larger community. Another may be one of several languages in a multilingual community where it may be related to a particular ethnic group, religious group or social class. It may on the other hand be the *lingua franca* or inter-community language. It may or may not have a standard form associated with official, educational and literary use. Some languages (Creoles) were originally Pidgins, simplified languages developed as a form of communication between colonizer and colonized. When they become the mother tongues of communities, the creolized pidgins become fully-fledged languages. Indeed these creoles are the most recent examples in history of the collective capacity of a community to fashion for itself a natural language.

Whatever we can learn about the languages we encounter amongst school pupils is likely to be of some value to us, like knowing, for example, that Urdu is written from right to left. We have moreover to learn not only the sociolinguistics of a language in its home base but also the circumstances in which London school pupils continue to use it. Is there some kind of community with its own institutions, formal and informal, in which the language is spoken (clubs, cafés, churches, fêtes and ceremonies)? Is its use restricted to the home? How is it used in the home — exclusively, for the discussion of certain topics, only to parents and the older folk? Is it a language in which literacy is common and significant? Are newspapers, books and films available?

There have been attempts to categorize languages on the basis of certain major sociolinguistic rather than linguistic principles. That is to say not on the internal features but on the external social function. Bell (1976) traces these attempts through the work of Stewart (1962, 1968), Fishman (1971) and Hymes (1971a). Table 3 which he provides serves as a useful guide to the multiplicity of languages and some of the terms in common use.

Table 3   from Bell, R. T. *Sociolinguistics*. Batsford, 1976

Sociolinguistic Typology 3

Attributes							Language Type	Example
1	2	3	4	5	6	7		
+	+	+	+	−	±	+	Standard	Standard English
+	−	+	+	−		+	Classical	K. James' Bible English
−	+	−	+	−	−	+	Vernacular	'Black English'
−	+	−	−	−	−	+	Dialect	Cockney
−	+	−	−	+	+	+	Creole	Krio
−	−	−	−	+	+	+	Pidgin	Neomelanesian
+	−	−	+	+	−	+	Artificial	'Basic English'
−	−	−	±	−	+	?	Xized Y	'Indian English'
−	−	−	−	+	+	−	Interlanguage	'A's English'
−	−	−	−	+	±	−	Foreigner Talk	'B's simplified English'

Key:
+ possession of attribute
− lack of attribute
± either + or −
? insufficient evidence

Attributes
1 Standardization
2 Vitality
3 Historicity
4 Autonomy
5 Reduction
6 Mixture
7 *De facto* norms

It is also relevant to the next section which discusses dialects. Languages are classified according to seven attributes which can briefly be described as follows.

1 *Standardization*. The language possesses codified norms which are accepted (grammars, dictionaries) especially in teaching.

2 *Vitality*. The language is still spoken in a community of native speakers.
3 *Historicity*. The speech community is concerned with the ancestry of its language.
4 *Autonomy*. The speakers consider their language to be distinct from other or other varieties.
5 *Reduction*. The language is an attenuated form of another variety (i.e. reduction of syntax, phonology and lexicon).
6 *Mixture*. The language is essentially not derived from sources outside itself. No language is of course 'pure' but there are periods of intense and periods of minimal borrowing.
7 *De facto norms*. There are norms of usage which, whether codified or not, are accepted in the community.

Table 3 illustrates the application of these attributes to kinds of English but it should be borne in mind that the award of a plus or minus is a matter of judgment and will give rise to many sharp disagreements. At this stage we put this model forward since it illustrates so well how much we need to know about any language. Any one of these seven attributes could be elaborated in great detail. This is precisely what Giles *et al* (1977) have done with the concept of *vitality*. This has a special relevance for us since they are concerned to elaborate the concept in a context of ethnolinguistic diversity. Furthermore they are asking the important question, 'What permits an ethnolinguistic community to survive as a group?'

The vitality of an ethnolinguistic group is that which makes a group likely to behave as a distinctive and active collective entity in inter-group relations.

This, of course, takes the idea of vitality much further. The elements which contribute to it are set out as a taxonomy (Fig. 1). The authors are mostly cautious about their model but quite rightly suggest that it can be usefully applied to language in inter-group relations.
There is no reason for us to be mesmerized by the apparent complexities and bewildering array of dimensions of language variety. The work we have referred to can be used critically and in a discriminating way; it can be tested against our own observations and knowledge.
Finally, there is the question of language attitudes. In the

Figure 1 **from Giles (ed)** *Language, Ethnicity and Intergroup Relations.*
Macmillan Press, 1977

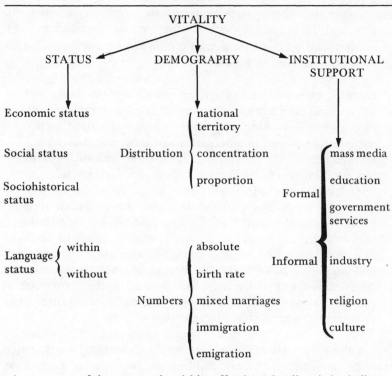

A taxonomy of the structural variables affecting ethnolinguistic vitality

end in education it is the critical question. We need to know the strength of a pupil's allegiance to his language remembering that this allegiance is itself dynamic, changing across time and from situation to situation. What evokes pride and warmth in the family circle or at a wedding perhaps may evoke embarrassment or even shame in another setting like school or a youth club. Some pupils visit the country of their family's origin quite frequently, others not at all. For the former the opportunity arises for them to observe and use the language in its home setting. They can appraise it more fully. Such an experience may strengthen their allegiance or weaken it. The attitudes of parents may, indeed do, often differ. The parents

27

may be eager for their children to learn Greek or Cantonese and press their children to attend out-of-school classes. The children may delight in this or bitterly resent it as a loss of liberty and an emphasis on their foreignness. As Khan (1978) has noted the parents' motives are complex, they may wish to sustain the language as a means of:

> ensuring communication with their children (in the linguistic and cultural sense), communication with grandparents etc. in the homeland, a prerequisite for marriage, settlement in the homeland, religious instruction and avoidance or resistance to Western culture and values . . . Work permit holders (e.g. Spanish, Turkish, Greek) have an added insecurity and uncertainty of place of final settlement. Whereas many Asian migrants have British passports, some categories of the population are orientated towards the homeland and others who planned to settle in Britain have become increasingly aware of the rejection and prejudice to be faced by their children. Certain exiled populations (the Eastern European, Cypriot and East African Asian) may in fact feel a greater concern than voluntary migrants to preserve traditions.

On the other hand, parents may take an integrationist stance and be anxious for their children to become as English as possible as soon as possible. Acquisition of linguistic competence would be seen as central to this process. In general, parents are likely to be under much less sustained pressure to perfect their English than their school-attending children whose inadequacies are likely to be underlined throughout the school day. The 'accommodation' theory propounded by Giles and his associates (Giles, *et al*, 1977) suggests:

> that people are continually modifying their speech with others so as to reduce or accentuate the linguistic (and hence social) differences between them depending on their perceptions of the interactive situation.

The matter does not end there, for we must also consider the attitudes of those who are not speakers of the language in question, the community at large, other pupils, teachers. Our tradition is certainly not a helpful one. In education we are stubbornly monolingual, although the first encouraging breaches have been made. Our reluctance to learn other languages is proverbial. This is to say no more than that the response to the fact that so many of our pupils speak another language has not in general been enthusiastic and may have taken the view (a long established one) that it was no business of schools to do anything about it except to ensure that it was replaced by English as soon as possible. Indeed to some, linguistic diversity is a heavy burden. As Haugen (1973) puts it:

> Those of us who love languages and have devoted our lives to learning and teaching them, and who find in language a source of novel delights and subtle experience, find it hard to put ourselves in the right frame of mind to understand the conception of language diversity as a curse.

In the last few years attitudes have begun to change. As communities have begun to organize themselves, they have articulated their views on language. As teachers have come through the initial shock of ethnically changed school populations and as young teachers have joined the profession blissfully unaware of a different dispensation, they have begun to respond to the need to know more about the range of languages they hear and hear about. There was scarcely a school we went into which did not contain its group of teachers already interested and committed and wanting to increase their knowledge and improve their practice.

6   DIVERSITY OF DIALECTS

Our study included recording the numbers of dialect speakers. Although it was to be expected that almost any English might occur (American, Australian, Geordie, Glaswegian etc.) two kinds of English were bound to have high frequency in our survey and each raised its own problems. They were London English and Caribbean dialects.

For a long time dialect study in English was based on the principle that dialect was essentially a regional matter so that an atlas might be compiled which mapped out the distribution of certain linguistic features. A huge volume has just appeared which represents the results of decades of labour of this kind (Orton *et al*, 1978). However, as we have indicated earlier, this would be impossible to do for London where a more complicated model than a map would be required. Indeed there is probably nowhere in England where a two-dimensional model would suffice. Certainly in London diverse social groups constantly interact and even residential patterns based on class or ethnicity would yield only small areas of homogeneity. This does not mean, on the other hand, that a prevailing dialect cannot be given a regional identity. Most people in England can identify a fully London (Cockney) speaker and many would identify the origin of a speaker whose speech contains a few features of London English. The vernacular speech of London will be spoken in the main by members of the working-class, although the situation is not as simple as that.

We have avoided defining dialect because linguists still disagree over knotty problems of definition. We all recognize that within Britain different kinds of English are spoken and these kinds of English differ from each other along the dimensions of their sound systems, their grammars and their lexicons. We also know that these kinds of English can be identified either geographically or socially. In some cases both criteria operate. It is customary to describe a dialect like Cockney as a 'low prestige' dialect, although this is a social not a linguistic judgment. Often it means no more than that people who consider their language to have high prestige have made the decision. A form of language which has low status to the outsider may be seen quite differently from the inside. A Cockney speaker may be quite satisfied with the way he speaks and not wish to change it. More usually, like all speakers of dialects who experience criticism from the powerful and educated, he is likely to be ambivalent about it, conceding, on the one hand, that it is not 'good English' and, on the other, resisting all efforts to make him change. Schools have frowned on regional working-class or rural speech and made efforts to suppress it. Indeed, universal education may have been the most potent force in making people lose confidence in their vernacular speech. London speech is socially tiered — but there are no sharp dividing lines between one tier and the next, as though it were neatly terraced. Intuitively we recognize the Cockney speaker, not only by his grammar, his accent and his vocabulary, but also by his style, voice quality and even the gestures which are integrated into his speech. He will also have an adundance of idioms and expressions of his own. It is a total style. Even among such readily recognized speakers there are differences. But in London a speaker may not be Cockney or something else. He can be more or less Cockney. Thus we may find in an area like Tottenham some seven or eight miles from the centre, many school pupils who sound like Cockney speakers until a total Cockney turns up in their midst. (This was exactly what happened in one group in a school.) What was the difference? In this area (mixed working-class and middle-class) some of the features and style of Cockney have been shed and the Standard form substituted. Within any individual we can detect differences from one situation to another. Teachers often say the children are bilingual when they observe the differences between playground and classroom. This does not meet the case: there is no sharply defined cut-off point, an *unambiguous discontinuity* (like, let us say, switching from English to Chinese or from Geordie to Standard).

It is Cockney in its full or modified form which most pupils from overseas encounter and the young ones grow up with. Their speech in English can be an *interlanguage*, a variety which is the speech of a second-language learner whose language still marks him out as a foreigner and is anywhere along a continuum from the first step to the one before the last.

The other area of great dialect complexity which is of great importance for London schools is the variety of West Indian dialects. We return to this in Chapter 3. At this stage we shall limit ourselves to some very general points. It took a long time for it to be appreciated in schools that the islands of the Caribbean have different dialects and that there are French, Portuguese and other Creoles. In London, Jamaican Creole is dominant so that other Creoles converge on it. In saying that one must repeat that the West Indian community in London has already developed a Jamaican Creole different from that spoken in Jamaica which we can call London Jamaican. No better example could be found of the relationship between language and identity than the use of London Jamaican by school pupils. There are numerous examples of black London-born pupils whose language differs in no way or very little from that of white London pupils. Many of these pupils, usually when they reach their early teens, learn London Jamaican and are very conscious of the symbolic nature of this act. More remarkably, a few white pupils under the influence of the peer-group have also learnt London Jamaican and we have encountered one example (there are probably many more) of a Nigerian London speaker who can also speak London Jamaican. This phenomenon of learning 'to talk black' is the more impressive since it often runs counter to wishes of parents who disapprove of 'bad talk'. Pupils who have in their repertoire a Caribbean Creole may in the school situation be reluctant to admit that they have it, such are the conflicting feelings and powerful attitudes which adhere to it.

The use of these two English dialects by black pupils is more like classical code switching but there are other complexities which must be taken into account. Some black pupils have some Creole features in their speech which remain concealed or suppressed unless they become deeply involved or drop their guard. Sometimes a single item of vocabulary or intonation will reveal this. We have also observed that quite often black pupils veer towards Standard more easily and more frequently than white London speakers. Tentatively we would suggest that their language experience being more varied than that of a typical Cockney makes their speech more pliant and open to a wider variety of language experience. This is not the obvious value judgment it seems to imply for it may be that the Cockney child's greater confidence in and satisfaction with his code is a source of strength while the West Indian child's awareness of pressure on his speech gives him flexibility at the price of confidence. These are very speculative comments but worth following up.

Apart from the example cited above we know little about the result of the interaction of London and West Indian vernaculars. We can say with some confidence, however, that the general expectation that the influence would all be one way (West Indian becoming London) will not be fulfilled in schools with large black populations.

We might look at London Cockney and London Jamaican within the framework suggested by Gumperz (1968). He proposes that the verbal repertoire of a community can be looked at in terms of (a) *linguistic range* and (b) *degree of compartmentalization*. 'Linguistic range refers to the internal language distance between constituent varieties' and 'compartmentalization to the sharpness with which varieties are set off from one another'. Linguistic range would apply to the distinct languages we have discussed above, whereas compartmentaliza-tion applies to our discussion of dialects. Gumperz offers this highly relevant description within this category:

> We speak of fluid repertoires, on the other hand, when there are transitions between adjoining vernaculars or when one speech style merges into another in such a way that it is difficult to draw clear borderlines.

Fluidity is indeed the hallmark of users of dialect in London schools, a fluidity which is both within and between individuals. This fluidity applies also to speakers of Standard who in certain areas are more numerous than might be expected in comprehen-sive schools, though they are never more than a strong minority. The influence of the peer-group is strong but not strong enough to do more in many cases than alter the vowel system and lead to the adoption of a small repertoire of peer-group phrases. In any case there is a form of London English which is well-known; it consists of Standard with London accent, i.e. mainly a London vowel system or the remnants of it.

Let us try to systematize what we have been discussing, bearing in mind that this cannot do more than suggest a basic pattern and that the dynamic reality is always too complex to be captured by the reductionism of diagrams and categories.

It is customary in sociolinguistic literature to speak of *code-switching* when someone changes from one dialect or language in his repertoire to another. The metaphor of switching is certainly appropriate for some dialect speakers whose change from one dialect to another is marked by sharp discontinuity, as it might be in a person who has acquired Standard through social and geographical mobility and revisits his childhood home. Intuitively we recognize the Cockney speaker not only by his grammar, his accent and lexicon, but also by his use of voice quality, his discourse style and the gestures integrated into the speech flow. He will also have an abundance of idioms and expressions of his own. Even among such readily recognized speakers there are differences. It is typical of urban diversity that a Cockney can adopt features of Standard in certain contexts; he can be more Cockney or less. In educational circles it is often declared policy to foster bidialectalism ('the language of the playground and the language of the school'). But what we are discussing is not code-switching. There is usually no unambiguous cut-off point at which London pupils can be said to have switched from Cockney to Standard. It would be better to talk of code-sliding along the continuum.

> ... to assume that each dialect has an autonomous grammar, and that bidialectal speakers shut off one grammar and switch on another, is just not credible in a case where most of the rules in the supposedly autonomous grammar would be exact duplicates of each other. (Fasold, 1975)

A quarter of a century ago it might have been plausible (forgetting minorities) to regard London speech as a *continuum*. A similar continuum might apply in other cities but this needs investigation.

Cockney →	Modified →	Standard- →	Standard-
(full dialect)	Cockney (adopting some features of Standard)	with-Cockney accent	with-Received Pronunciation

This continuum would represent the main categories for certain speakers but would also represent the choices in a repertoire which could be differentially drawn upon by the speaker. The more distant the category the less likely is it that it would be included in a speaker's repertoire. The adjacent categories are most readily available. We have now to accommodate new varieties of English which do not fit into that continuum.

The most complex problem remains the categorization of West Indian speech. The questionnaire (Appendix 2) shows how it was solved in practical decision-making terms. Of course, there are Londoners of West Indian origin who are in precisely the same position as other London children somewhere on the London continuum. Once that is said the possibilities are numerous, basically because there is a dynamic, highly mobile relationship between varieties of West Indian English and varieties of London English.

These are the starting points:

(i) one of the Caribbean English-based Creoles;
(ii) a Caribbean standard

(iii) anywhere between (i) and (ii) on the Creole continuum;*
(iv) London Jamaican

The major complexity arises from the fact that a London West
Indian pupil's language is influenced by the interaction of two
continua thus:

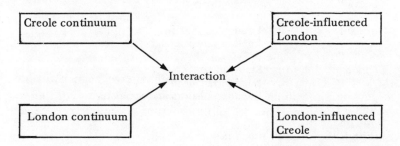

The West Indian element in their speech may derive from any
part of the Creole continuum and the London element from any
part of the London continuum. Thus the range of possibilities is
enormous. A further complexity is added by the unpredicted
emergence of London Jamaican. In general, like speakers
on the London continuum, West Indians slide from one position
to another but with a wider range of choices. However it is
important to bear in mind that in this intricate picture London
Jamaican occupies a unique position for London school pupils.

If we take a monodialectal view of the kinds of English
which we might find in a London school, then this list would
be comprehensive:

Standard
London (Cockney)
Non-London British Isles dialects
Overseas dialects of English   (a)   English-based Creoles
                                (b)   Others
London Jamaican
Interlanguage

But that list fails to plot possible relationships between the
varieties when we look at them from the point of view of the

*Edwards (1979) 'The linguistic situation in the West Indies can best be described in
terms of a continuum with broad Creole at one end and standard English at the other.
Each speaker will command a span on the continuum rather than simply occupying
a point on it.' (p.16)

35

individual speaker. Table 4 below shows how we see some of the major possibilities.

Table 4

Dominant Dialect or Variety	CODE-SLIDING moving towards
Standard	(i)→ London
	(ii)→ London Jamaican
London	(i)→ Standard
	(ii)→ London Jamaican
	(iii)→ London Jamaican and Standard
Non-London British Isles	(i)→ London
	(ii)→ Standard
	(iii)→ London and Standard
English-based Creoles	(i)→ London Jamaican
	(ii)→ London
	(iii)→ Standard
	(iv)→ London and Standard
	(v)→ London and Standard and London Jamaican
Interlanguage	(i)→ London
	(ii)→ London and Standard
	(iii)→ Standard

In addition there is code-switching:

London continuum ⟶ London Jamaican

7 BILINGUALISM

Of the various issues we raised in this introduction this is in one respect the most important, simply because nationally and educationally we have very little experience of bilingualism. Very few teachers are bilingual in most senses of the term or have any deep awareness of what it means either to be bilingual or to be a member of a bilingual community. To be the speaker of a language other than English is also to be a member of a minority group and possibly to participate in a minority culture. This too is an experience which many teachers have not undergone. We draw attention to this not in order to apportion blame (which in most cases would be ridiculous) but to draw attention to how much most of us have to learn about the language and experience of pupils in London, and that we have to learn the hard way since we cannot simply internalize the experience of others overnight.

There is now a considerable literature on bilingualism though the term covers a wide range of relationships both within individuals and in different kinds of communities. For our purposes no hard and fast definition of bilingualism is helpful. 'The best way to deal with . . . variations in definitions would seem to be to recognize that bilingualism is not an all-or-none property, but is an individual characteristic that may exist to degrees from minimal competency to complete mastery of more than one language.' (Hornby, 1977.) Though the perfect bilingual is one who has equal mastery at the highest level of two languages, this is probably an ideal which no one attains. Even perfect balance at any level must be either rare or impossible. Almost all bilinguals have a dominant language — the one they think in, feel more completely themselves in. So it is that in our study we differentiate between those who are English speakers but have some competence in another language and those who are speakers of another language with some degree of competence in English. Another asymmetry in bilingualism is the use of one language for one set of situations, the other for another. In London we are not dealing with long established communal bilingualism of the recent (historically speaking) newcomer. Thus the bilingualism of the London school will take many different forms. The sharpest division will be between those pupils whose first language is English and those whose second language is English. The former will have different degrees of mastery over the second (non-English) language and vice versa for the latter. We must also recognize that some pupils are in a less fortunate state than the simple dichotomy we have given. They may have native-like mastery of neither language ('semi-lingualism'). Attention has also been drawn to the deceptive nature of some people's achievement in a second language. They may achieve a fluent everyday use of the language which though still 'foreign' suggests they are at home in it. School pupils may give the impression that school lessons present them with no problems of comprehension or expression, when, in fact, there are nuances being lost and more basic features, certain structures for instance, still elude them. There is no need to exaggerate this: the other side of the coin is that 'on the basis of partial information . . . one can usually form a correct hypothesis about that which someone is trying to communicate' (Macnamara, 1966).

There has been lengthy discussion and considerable research which attempt to resolve whether there are cognitive advantages or disadvantages attributable to bilingualism. At one time it was confidently believed that the two language systems would interfere with thought processes, thus hindering development in general and schooling in particular. There is, however, a mounting body of findings to suggest that, in the first place, the question is not as simple as it looks; secondly that *given certain provisos* it can be an asset which puts the bilingual at a cognitive advantage (Lambert, 1977). An even stronger case can be made out for believing that bilinguals and monolinguals do not differ in any way in their basic thought processes. It should be clear that if we are discussing children's success in learning in school then bilinguals may be less successful for reasons which have nothing to do with their bilingualism as such (prejudice, failure to accommodate them culturally, etc.).

Bilingualism does not necessarily imply biculturalism. A school pupil who attains a high degree of proficiency in learning to speak, read and write French will, in all likelihood, have little or no sense of either cultural ambiguity or duality, although it is arguable that to attain that level some shift of cultural viewpoint is necessary. The pupils we are considering are in quite a different situation. Their proficiency in one of the languages may be much lower than that of a school language learner but their biculturalism much more profound. Many of them will, to a greater or lesser degree, be living two cultures. A Chinese girl may live for part of her time in a Chinese culture and part in a British one and part in a mixture of the two if her home has undergone a degree of Anglicization. The Chinese culture will in any case be that form of it which has developed in this country. She will not only be absorbing cultural meanings for the same activities, such as eating, but possibly taking up values and attitudes which have no analogies in the two cultures. It does not follow that the two cultures match perfectly the two languages. A Jewish culture has persisted outside the speaking of Yiddish. Nevertheless, language is a highly salient dimension of ethnic identity. It is a highly explicit carrier of cultural meaning. Put very simply, a Greek child may feel Greek when speaking English but much more Greek when speaking Greek. Does this mean that bilinguals must inevitably feel a sense of conflict, of divided allegiances or, perhaps, neither? Lambert (1977) considers the results of a study (Child, 1943) of second generation Italians in the United States which shows that they could be divided into three groups. One group rebelled against their Italian background and made themselves as American as possible, another rejected American culture and championed their Italian identity and a third, caught in the crossfire, tried unsuccessfully to avoid ethnic allegiance of any kind. Lambert is surprised that no group emerged which had developed a sense of allegiance to both cultures. He compares this with his own study of French-American adolescents. He found that there were those who showed a preference for American culture and denied the value of knowing French. Their English was better than their French. Then there were those who wished to be identified as French whose French, especially spoken French, was better than their English. A third group were ambivalent and they were retarded in both languages compared to other groups. However, there was a fourth group which had 'an open-minded non-ethnocentric view of people and an aptitude for language learning' and which became skilled in both languages, having achieved 'a comfortable bicultural identity'. Lambert sees great hope for the future in bicultural bilinguals who are likely to become the banner-bearers of multi-culturalism.

We have done no more than touch on these matters because they demand fuller treatment than we can give them in these pages. We hope we have said enough to show that bilingualism leads us to the difficult issues of ethnicity, culture and identity. These are issues to which teachers need to give sustained attention in all schools, but especially in schools which are centres of linguistic and cultural diversity.

Chapter 3   The survey: design and findings

1   PLANNING THE STUDY

A survey is a practical enterprise. We have attempted up to this point to show how much more is involved than arithmetic and to sketch the kind of thinking which had to enter our collective awareness before and while that enterprise was taking shape. This chapter will attempt to describe how the survey took shape and will present the results which emerged from it. We set ourselves three principal tasks:

1   Gathering information about *which languages were spoken by what proportions of pupils.* The main dimensions of diversity would be (a) UK based vernaculars (b) overseas dialects of English and (c) languages other than English. We knew this would in many instances require difficult decision-making.

2   Gathering information about *the extent to which particular languages and dialects were spoken, the strength of dialectal features, literacy in Standard English, in other languages and even dialect.* This information clearly called for more obviously qualitative judgment.

3   *The correlation of information obtained from (1) and (2)* which would suggest additional conclusions and/or point to further study, e.g. differences between boys and girls; whether literacy in English is helped or hindered by literacy in another language. These possibilities were suggested by the data though there are, of course, other themes which cry out for enquiry. But this is a relatively unresearched area and this aspect of the survey we thought might be suggestive to studies which must inevitably follow ours, both locally and nationally.

To say that language diversity is in this country unresearched academically is not the same as saying that very little is known about it. Many teachers have considerable knowledge at classroom level of the languages and cultures of their pupils. Although this knowledge is rarely systematized in schools, it is nonetheless the base on which many schools could undertake their own surveys and more detailed studies than more broad-based surveys could hope to attempt. For us, embarking on our study and conscious of the limitations of our own history, there was no doubt that this was a rich resource to be drawn upon. On the other hand, our experience of collaborative research on language in inner-city schools made us equally certain that we needed to be responsive to teachers' ideas, suggestions and expressed needs. Both the design of the study and the selection of particular schools rested on these strategic considerations.

It follows, then, that a number of schools with whom we were already in active collaboration became the earliest for sampling and investigation. Three of them became the pilot schools in which the instruments we were to design were tested. More important perhaps was our decision about methods. We resisted the temptation (a strong one given the constraints of time and resources) to opt for as much as possible as quickly as possible and decided instead to retain the well-tried principles of cooperation which we were using in our work and adapt them to this exercise. These four features were therefore adopted:

(a) the information would be gathered first class by class and then school by school
(b) the eliciting and compiling of data would be a task jointly undertaken by teachers and researchers, difficulties being resolved through discussion
(c) the data having been processed would be fed back to a school as soon as possible
(d) the survey in schools would be preceded by briefing sessions and followed up by meetings which would explore the implications of the results.

We hoped the information would be of immediate use to schools and would stimulate discussion of policy and practice. We, for our part, would learn directly from the teachers with whom we were working. These processes would increase accuracy and

41

sensitivity of the information obtained.

The second influence on the design was the nature of the information we sought. We wanted more than overall numbers of speakers of different languages and dialects and at the same time knew that we had to settle for less than a full sociolinguistic enquiry. The question for us was then (as we saw our questionnaire growing to formidable proportions): how far could we incorporate qualitative considerations? We had in mind such matters as the extent to which languages were spoken and levels of literacy. We knew this would place heavier demands on the teachers and yet make their participation a rich and fuller experience. In a conceptually difficult area our instruments had both to inform and arouse interest.

For these reasons we gave special attention to the questionnaire (Appendix 2) and the introduction (Appendix 1) to it. An interested reader would probably find that the best way of making them come to life would be to try to use them with a single class. Although the questionnaire must be judged as the key tool of the research, we had also to decide on the methods for gathering information. We needed to take a single starting point which would be accessible to teachers. We began with *the language of the pupil in the classroom.* This was not without its problems. Most obviously, the language used by pupils may not be their mother tongue. For some it may be a second or third language. Also, as many teachers pointed out, the English used in the classroom may be a Sunday-best version, as used to the teacher, especially when compared to the English used outside or in the peer group. Yet there are also advantages in beginning from this point in the pupil's classroom language. An estimation by the teachers is allowed for, based not only on everyday knowledge but actually listening to the pupil's speech. Our belief is that much of the interest and educative potential of the survey has derived from this demand. Just as important, starting with the pupil's language in the classroom permits a weighted and dynamic picture of dialect, bidialectalism and bilingualism to be formed — one that is potentially more accurate and delicate than a mere count of different dialects and languages could have yielded. Such at any rate was our beginning. Teachers were asked initially for broad judgments and allocations entered in different sections of the questionnaire. These were then refined, where possible, by means of supplementary questions and answers. By making an overall

42

sectionalization the basis for this initial allocation it was then possible to restrict the number of further questions to those relevant to the initial allocation. (See Introduction to questionnaire, p.151, Note 3 which asks the data-collector to place the pupil's speech in *either* Section A, Great Britain based English *or* Section B overseas dialects and languages.)

We then gave consideration to methods of gathering the data. At no point was it envisaged that a teacher would be sitting down with a child and simply going through the questions as a one-to-one sustained investigation. Such a procedure would have been both to set at risk the sensitivity and accuracy of the information we sought and to deny the educative potential in an exercise to which, as time went on, we felt increasingly committed. So we were reliant for our procedures on the judgment of the teachers with whom we were working and in due course learnt to couple with this another support — the interest of the pupils for the exercise itself. The central technique, as it turned out, was the group interview, begun typically with questions about language a long way from the information which we finally sought, but intended to encourage the flow of interest and to involve pupils in talking about language. Often enough this was supplemented with material, for example in an overseas dialect or a language other than English, or a book of examples of different languages with information about them. Sometimes, such interviews were linked specifically to the curriculum. The data-collectors kept notes of the facts which emerged from discussion including any matters which raised doubts in their minds. These were then pursued further by whatever means seemed suitable or accessible: school records, teachers' knowledge, a further discussion with an individual pupil or listening to tape. We worked from the principle that the process of enquiry should be involving, un-threatening and, above all, positive. Where children were reluctant to vouchsafe information about themselves, it was important that this right be protected. But in practice such reluctance was very rare. The charge of prying unduly is one that we are sensitive about and sought at all costs to avoid. But the central point concerns not the avoidance of insensitive clumsiness, important though that is, but the necessity to work in this way in gathering the information which we sought.

To sum up then: in a first investigation of language diversity, undertaken within the London area, we sought to gather both relatively straightforward information of a head-counting kind and other more qualitative data, at least sufficient to allow some estimate of the extent of bidialectalism, bilingualism and biliteracy and perhaps suggestive of future areas of study which might repay further investigation. Two principal influences on the design of the study and on our way of working were the concern to forward a school/research collaboration which would be helpful to both sides and an accompanying awareness of the kinds of procedures which were necessary for gathering information of the kind we sought. Our central methodology may be described as a survey modified by the influences which we have described.

We defer to a later section details of the resultant sample, variables and data. Here we may merely pick up one or two further points. We might of course have done it differently. Our view of the linguistic precision of some of the information returned is straightforward. A first, bold step for teachers and researchers alike was needed. There is a relatively clear distinction between levels of comparative certainty in the information elicited. We may be reasonably certain, for example, about whether an additional language is spoken by a pupil, even if we are less sure about the degree of the pupil's fluency. The form of a survey creates certain demands and limitations which would not be present in a case study or in a detailed investigation of a handful of pupils. A balance has to be maintained between the delicacy of questions asked and what is practicable within the constraints of time available to teachers and the general compass of what is possible. We have tried, at any rate, to avoid some errors to which rapid gathering of information within this area is prone. Above all, we have tried to make a beginning in the design of an instrument, the questionnaire, which avoids errors deriving from a basic assumption of monodialectalism or monolingualism. Some of the more familiar terms, e.g. 'the pupil's mother tongue' or the 'language of the home' fail to do this justice. It is clear that there is no single, mother tongue or language of the home for the many Greek pupils who speak Greek all the time to one parent (who is perhaps still not a very fluent English speaker), English some of the time to the other parent (except at family, communal occasions, perhaps) and English *all* of the time with brothers and sisters at school. That is just to give one example. Others could be multiplied, with important sub-cultural differences,

44

and are just as relevant to dialect-speakers.

A middle course is always a difficult one to steer. We do not deny the value of one or two simple questions about language diversity and a quick mass return of information; and had we limited our enquiry more sharply we might have covered more ground. But we were convinced of the need, on the one hand to take the total range of diversity as the point of study, on the other to develop an approach which recognized multi-lingualism and multi-dialectalism as a central experience, at any rate in London schools. Our concern has been not so much with the question: 'What is the pupil's mother tongue?' as with the broader question: 'What languages and dialects have the pupils in London schools available to use, how often and for what purposes and with what facility?' The range and interaction is the crucial experience with which schools have to deal.

2 THE SAMPLE

So far we have suggested the influence behind the choices as to ways of working which we made and our general orientation. We now address the more fundamental questions in any research. Put simply, the reader has the right to know in advance the scope and strengths and weaknesses of the information being offered to him. In the details of schools and data which we now give our intention is to make this plain. The bare facts first:

No. of pupils	4,600 (boys 46%: girls 54%)
No. of schools	28 (all secondary: 10 single sex 18 mixed)
Age group	11–12 years (i.e. first-year pupils)
% of age group	14%

We have called our survey a modified survey, modified firstly in its way of working in close collaboration with schools, secondly in the delicacy of judgments which were sought where teachers felt it possible to supply an answer. We must also make it clear that it was never our intention to achieve anything approaching a comprehensive picture of language diversity in the total range of London. Clearly such a task was beyond us. It was necessary to sample and select.

The 4,600 children in the first year of twenty-eight schools who constitute our final sample represent approximately 14% of the age group. We had hoped to reach a target of 20 per cent of secondary schools (forty in number) which would have justified the claim of representative status for the sample. The sample is composed moreover of a single age group. We had our reasons for choosing the age group we did. Principal among these were that 11/12 year old population offered the nearest to a midpoint in the pupils' school career which it was practicable for us to take. It also left the maximum opportunity for later follow-up, either by us, if circumstances permitted, or by the school, acting on information which the experience of participation might make available. But restriction to any single age group in sampling linguistic diversity poses obvious limitations. On the one hand, a sample taken earlier, might have caught more speakers nearer to a language used in infancy or at a time when the influence of the home was more dominant. On the other, there is some experience to suggest that interest in a language other than English, potentially part of a speaker's cultural inheritance, or (for example) in patois, may be a development which flowers during the secondary school years for some. Earlier, such accomplishment may merely seem diversionary. Both the restriction to a single age range and the finally unrepresentative nature of the sample need to be taken into account in interpreting overall distributions. There is also an additional point, most forcefully put by a group of teachers at one of our research conferences. A sample freezes. It catches a moment in time and, in the case of this sample, a moment within pupils' school careers. Yet an important dimension of our understanding of language diversity needs to be over time, both within individual history and within the larger social history surrounding the individual.

So we shall be looking at distributions arising from a less than representative sample. It is, nonetheless, a very substantial sample. Such a sample suggests the dimensions of diversity even if it does not present a wholly comprehensive picture. We need to add too that we were unable to draw the sample either against the background of predictions of expected diversity from a source within the local authority or on any of the usual bases for achieving randomness. The absence of predictions is a technical point. Had we been able to arrive at a set of expected totals for the different language populations in the sample, a

46

basis would have been open for calculating the significance of totals which we actually found. But of course at the time of undertaking the survey no such basis for estimating expected totals was available either to us or to the local authorities with whom we were in contact. The randomness of the sample is an equally important question. In the end we were defeated in achieving this by time and resources available to us and by the exigencies in the schools. It was in the end more important that a school wanted to work with us and could manage within its own schedule the necessary space for the conduct of a relatively substantial operation, than that we were able to preserve an optimally random pattern of selection of every school. We had, in any case, our doubts from the beginning about whether a numerical randomness achieved by moving through a list was a procedure appropriate to the very uneven layering of language diversity through different areas of London. With all the time in the world, a grand design would have been both to take an initial 20 per cent sample on a random basis, with later sub-sampling for particular language groupings. Such a design, though in our heads, was beyond our scope to achieve.

So our sample is somewhat accidental in composition. We found ourselves in touch through the year with schools contacted though various sources. One origin, as we have described, was the original Language in the Inner City project, another the advice of colleagues or of the Inspectorate in the ILEA. We are grateful for such help. Gradually too, as the year went on, we even found schools approaching us from their own interest in undertaking the work. We also made contact with a borough outside the ILEA — as a check, bearing in mind the notion that in a borough containing far less secondary schools than in the ILEA it would thereby be very much easier to achieve a sample of representative proportions. On a rough and subjective basis we tried, as we accumulated schools to preserve representation, on the one hand, of known dimensions of language diversity and, on the other, a geographical spread. But we cannot know objectively whether we succeeded, nor can we say definitely that proportions between different language groupings, for example, proportions of Standard as against London speakers, speakers of West Indian patois as against speakers of a South Asian language and so on — have any probability of being repeated were a different sample to be taken.

As a picture of diversity in London schools, then, our sample

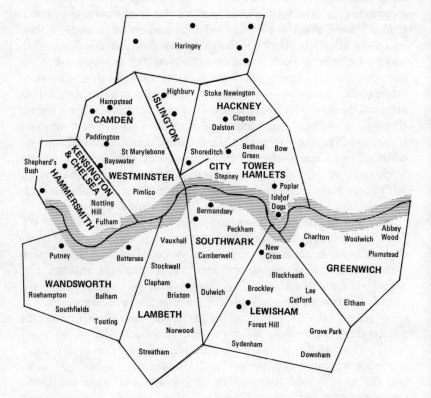

Haringey

Highbury

Hampstead

Stoke Newington

HACKNEY

CAMDEN

Clapton

ISLINGTON

Dalston

Paddington

St Marylebone

Shoreditch

Bethnal
Green

Bow

Bayswater

Shepherd's
Bush

KENSINGTON
& CHELSEA

WESTMINSTER

CITY

TOWER
HAMLETS

Stepney

HAMMERSMITH

Notting
Hill

Pimlico

Poplar

Isle)of
Dogs

Fulham

Bermondsey

Abbey
Wood

Peckham

Charlton

Woolwich

Putney

Vauxhall

SOUTHWARK

Battersea

Camberwell

New
Cross

Plumstead

Stockwell

Blackheath

GREENWICH

WANDSWORTH

Clapham

Brockley

Lee

Roehampton

Balham

Brixton

Dulwich

Catford

Eltham

Southfields

LEWISHAM

Tooting

LAMBETH

Forest Hill

Grove Park

Norwood

Sydenham

Downham

Streatham

is almost certainly weighted in some degree, nor is it in the technical sense objectively reliable. There is good reason to believe that our sample has some biases — towards North London, likely to favour for example Greek and Turkish speakers and perhaps, as we move further from the inner city centre, speakers of Standard English; also a probable under-representation of South Asian languages. Finally, while the sample would certainly reflect major groupings, very small groupings might have been missed altogether. We have said so much to keep the record straight and claim no more for our survey than it merits. But in meeting our obligations we wish to emphasize that we have not been engaged in impressionistic journalism. Our sample is a large one. To know the central facts of diversity in twenty-eight schools is a solid foundation on which to build and that extension can begin at any time.

There are other imbalances, actually or potentially significant, which we set out schematically with comments below.

(a) Girls outnumber boys by 8% (boys 46%; girls, 54%)
(b) Girls at single sex school, 27% at 4 schools
(c) Number of mixed schools, 18

Comment   These differences by gender and type of school could have had some effect on overall totals and distributions.

(d) Contributions of schools to total sample:
No school contributes more than 6%
No school contributes less than 2%
9 schools contribute 47%
6 of the smallest schools contribute 11%

Comment   A school or two with, for example, a very high proportion of one language group might distort overall totals. This too is unlikely to have exerted a strong effect on the results. However, school to school differences are, indeed, very marked and we return to this question in Chapter 4. (See pp. 98–105.)

(e) Variables not included in survey (i) social class, occupational group of parents, family size, position in family, education of parents etc. (ii) overall measures of ability

(iii) culture, nationality and ethnicity

Comment   We kept the focus sharply on language and were
not concerned with whether pupils think of
themselves or are thought of by others as
British or something else, the time elapsed since
arrival in this country, whether they were likely
to be leaving in the near future etc. The force
of these *caveats* is that there are no simple
conclusions to be drawn from our data about
relationships between the linguistic resources
of the pupils and their general educational
achievement.

3   DATA AND DATA-PROCESSING

As for the data, these have been drawn, in the end, from
responses of teachers to thirty-four questions, intended to
help them to allocate as speakers children in the classes which
they taught. The range of such questions, together with identifying information and a number of summary checks generated
a total of forty-four variables. Qualitative judgments, for
example as to the strength of dialectal features, were expressed
as numbered values within many of these variables. This is the
scope of the technical data with which computerization was
approached. Data were recorded in the first instance on class-
based record sheets, which in turn supplied the data for calcula-
tion of proportions of speakers of different languages and
dialects by school. Tables of this kind were calculated by hand
and returned to the schools during the year in which the
research was conducted.

At a later stage the data were transferred from these record
sheets to computer coding sheets, set out by pupil, in classes, in
schools and cards punched on this basis. Our data then are
essentially distributional — frequencies within different language
variables, percentage proportions of one sort of speaker as
against another, frequencies and percentage proportions in
certain values. Some correlation and cross-tabulation between
variables has been possible. Given the limitations in the data
we have described above, work of this kind has been kept to
a minimum and is always offered speculatively. Nevertheless,

in a section which has perhaps overstressed the edges of the data, it needs to be said that the picture which can be assembled is wholly fascinating. To this we turn.

4 WHO SPEAKS WHAT?

Most of the 4,600 11/12 year olds spoke English, but then that is neither surprising nor is it the whole story. On the one hand children converge as they must on a common language within the classroom with which to talk to each other and to share learning. On the other, different dialects of English and different capacities in the language coexist, often unnoticed within the overall classroom concentration on communicating with each other. And beneath the surface, for the most part, of most classrooms lie further resources and capacities for a substantial number of children, which are nevertheless not irrelevant because they are for the most part unemployed. Our intention then, as teachers and researchers, was to draw closer — to arrive at estimated proportions of speakers of different Great Britain based dialects of English and of overseas languages and dialects. These three axes cover the possibilities, yet the divisions in the classroom, of course, are not so clear cut. Convergence between dialects of English, Great Britain or overseas based, bidialectalism and bilingualism are typical, not unusual in the linguistic interaction which the teacher meets.

Monolingualism, bidialectalism, bilingualism
Our questionnaire bore on this mixture in a number of inter-related ways.

1 *Initially it asked for discrete categorizations* where possible into A speakers of a Great Britain based dialect of English or B speakers of an overseas dialect of English or language other than English. The criterion for this first division was simply enough stated, though not always easy to hear in practice: whether the speech of the pupil in the classroom carried identifiable features deriving ultimately from an overseas dialect or overseas language. Only speakers who are unambiguously and without trace speakers of a Great Britain based dialect were allocated to Section A. Others were placed in Section B.

2   *The second step was to allocate within sub-sections of Section A or Section B* — either as a speaker of a London, a non-London regional or Standard variety of English (Section A) or as a speaker of an overseas dialect or language (Section B). So the category 'speaker of a Great Britain based dialect of English' was first more narrowly defined to exclude the presence of overseas features and then subdivided into three possibilities. Within the categories relating to speaker of an overseas dialect of English and a language other than English, the further question, 'Which dialect?' or 'Which language?' was entered simply from information, where possible, derived from the pupils and reference to a languages and dialects list.

3   *A third step related to bidialectal and bilingual pupils* and also to those who might not fit very easily into the simple set of divisions so far described. This was the possibility of entering further languages and dialects which might be spoken by the pupil. This possibility applied of course whether pupils were allocated to Section A or to Section B. It also eased the sometimes arbitrary nature of initial allocation. Thus a bilingual child, speaking English fluently but an additional language as well, could be allocated confidently as a British speaker with the fact of his/her bilingualism at a later stage. The same would apply to a London/Jamaican speaker, whose Caribbean features in some contexts would be virtually non-existent. Such a speaker could be allocated either in Section B or in Section A, where there was genuine doubt; but in either case an essential item in the repertoire of his/her speech would be caught by the survey.

We have set out the details of these three moves made by the teacher in allocating the speech of particular pupils, on the one hand as an indication of the way we sought to meet in our questionnaire the complexity of the linguistically diverse and linguistically mixed classroom, on the other, because such categories of recording underlie the distributions which we have to present. Thus an answer to the question 'Who speaks what?' can be presented either flatly by carrying forward sub-totals in the categories along the three principal axes; or more intricately by the consideration of questions of bidialectalism and bilingualism, of further languages and dialects spoken. This question is of more than academic interest. Not only is incorporation of a decent understanding of the bilingual and bidialectal speaker a crucial step to take in our picture of language in the classroom, but also an understanding of the pupils' speech based only on the speech heard in the classroom, without further consideration of additional resources, might seriously underestimate the extent of diversity present in London schools. Yet this must be the position of many teachers who, through time or uncertainty in a fairly complex terrain, operate straightforwardly on the basis of the classroom language they hear, without setting out to make some more explicit description of the language in their class — an enterprise, it should be added, which offers possibilities, collaboration and mutual learning between classes and teacher which could develop well beyond the apparently narrow starting point.

Table 5   Proportions in the main language groupings
(excluding considerations of bidialectalism and bilingualism)

	%	%
Great Britain based dialects of English		84
London dialect	67	
Non-London dialect	2	
Standard	15	
Overseas dialect		10
Language other than English		6

It is necessary then to qualify the ground plan given in Table 5 in order to arrive at a more accurate picture. On the one hand, pupils allocated in the first instance to Section A but who also spoke a further language or dialect of English constitute a proportion (14 per cent) very nearly as great as all those allocated to Section B. On the other, all but a very small number of pupils allocated to Section B (3 per cent) were judged to be perfectly adequate speakers of English, even though their English might bear within it some traces of overseas features. *This range and extent of bilingualism and bidialectalism is one central finding of our survey.* To those familiar with London schools the extent may not be unexpected. What did surprise us was the degree to which fluency in another language or dialect was often wholly undeclared in the pupil's classroom speech. Table 6 displays a fuller picture of diversity.

Table 6   Proportions in the main language groupings
(expressed as proportions of monolingual, bidialectal and bilingual speakers)

	%	%
Monolingual speakers with use of a Great Britain based dialect of English only		70
London	56	
Non-London	2	
Standard	12	
Bidialectal speakers with some use both of a Great Britain and overseas based dialect of English		14
Great Britain and Caribbean	13	
Great Britain and other overseas dialect	1	
Bilingual speakers with some use both of English and a language other than English		14
Overseas dialect dominant		1
Overseas language dominant		1

As a first step in the question: 'Who speaks what?' we have taken, then, the major language groupings within our sample and immediately qualified these to indicate the extent of bidialectalism and bilingualism which these conceal; and it is a consistent thread in our argument that it is with this rich picture that we need to operate both descriptively and educationally. A small number of speakers of languages other than English, in initial stages as learners of English as a second language, do not justify a policy which exclusively emphasizes special English teaching provision. Bidialectalism and bilingualism on this scale raise questions of a quite different order, not merely for the teaching of English but for all teachers and educators. Our next step though is specification in more detail. Between them, as we shall see, the pupils in our sample spoke some *twenty different varieties of Great Britain based English, together with forty-two different overseas dialects of English and fifty-five named world languages.*

Great Britain based dialects of English (Tables 5 and 7)

Among the Great Britain based dialects of English, London speakers, not surprisingly constitute the major sub-population (56 per cent of the total sample). Even so straightforward a finding is not without its complexity. Nobody speaks real Cockney if you ask them — or practically none of the children whom we talked to, anyway. Whether in dockland or the outer reaches of North London, Cockney, we were invariably told, was more richly, or more deeply or more idiomatically spoken elsewhere. Unmistakably, though, the children who told us this were London and not Standard speakers. 'London' clearly enough is a rough and ready term, masking differences between north and south, east and west, from area to area, and between occupations. That said, the term seemed, in the event, workable enough and to cover a range of non-Standard speech, familiar enough to London teachers, employed by some indigenously and by others by adoption.

A qualititative distinction, which we made in the questionnaire, aimed partly at this variety, but most directly on the question of the convergence of London and Standard English. This is easiest to describe as a difference between strong and weak versions of both dialects. The background to such a formula is of course convergence as a more general process within the total variety characteristic of London schools. London speech moving towards Standard or Standard towards London may seem a fine distinction to make, and indeed was one of the points most recurrently taken up at briefing meetings with teachers. Yet there is evidence within our sample that something is reflected by such an apparently vague categorization. Firstly it proved usable, and at a common sense level is, after all, a judgment which we are making much of the time. Also the connection between a proportion of weak-London speakers and Standard speakers is on the whole reflected in the balance returned by individual schools. A higher proportion of weak-London speakers would be expected in schools possessing, as not all schools do, a substantial number of Standard speakers.

This is, with no more than one exception, the case.

Speakers of a non-London regional dialect of English, by origin, who have been pupils for some time in London schools, are of course also likely to converge on London or Standard English. The range of such dialects is potentially wide, though pupils of Irish, Welsh and Scots origin form some of the obvious groupings. A total of 2 per cent of the total numbers of pupils in our sample spoke between them some twenty different dialects. This is not a massive total, but such different ways of speaking are part of the identity of these pupils and a part of the total richness of language to be found in an inner-city area. These are regional speakers then accommodating both to Standard and to the local London vernacular. In practice, our design allows less delicately for speakers of this sort than for some others, principally because they were of secondary interest as a matter of detailed record. We confined our attention to a scale based on the strength of non-London features of speech. But the range of possibilities is more complex than that. Scots speakers, in particular, in our subsequent experience, seemed often to be bidialectal and able to shift at will between a London speech in the classroom and a wholly distinct Scots used with relatives. It is unnecessary to pursue the full range of possibilities here. It is merely worth recording that this was a less developed aspect of our investigation which might repay further study.

Table 7   Strength of dialectal features within Great Britain based dialects of English

	Strong distinctive %	Weak converging %
London	49	51
Standard	38	62
Non-London regional	6	94

Recapitulating what is more a general impression than a finding strictly supported by numerical evidence, one or two features about the Great Britain based dialects of English stand out. Firstly, there is a high order of convergence, not confined as we have already noted, to Great Britain based dialects. There is a similar point to be made about Caribbean speakers as well. Yet, for all that, Standard English remains surprisingly distinct. Standard English is sporadically rather than thinly spread through our schools. Only nine possessed more than twenty speakers throughout their first year and there are some where there were no Standard speakers recorded at all. Moreover, in classrooms where London and Standard do coexist, even though there may be some convergence of accent, the social origins of the two speeches keep them, in all essentials somehow oddly distinct. Behind this rests, we are aware, a sociology on which, within this sample, we have no evidence. A corresponding point is the power and persistence of London speech. It remains the central and most prevalent fact about London classrooms. That is not merely stating the obvious. It needs remembering and carrying forward as we consider the even greater complexity introduced by overseas based dialects and languages other than English.

Overseas dialects of English
Within the sixty-five varieties of English reflected in our sample, pupils with some use of an overseas dialect of English, often bidialectal, constitute a proportion of 15 per cent (712 pupils). The majority of this sub-group (71 per cent) derive, over several generations from Jamaica. Rather over 17 per cent, however, were from families from thirteen other regions of the Caribbean and the South American sub-continent; while a further 6 per cent (42 pupils) came from seven different parts of Africa, from Canada and the USA, and from Australia and New Zealand. The preponderance of dialects of English originating in the Caribbean is not of course surprising. It is worth noting though that a quarter of the pupils speaking, to some extent, an overseas dialect of English were either from the Eastern Caribbean or from other parts of the world. West Indian dialects are not uniform, nor are they the only overseas dialects of English spoken in London schools.

No mere survey/questionnaire research can replace the detailed study which is needed both of Creoles in the West Indian islands (and South American sub-continent) and of the significance of forms of Jamaican and other patois as they are being developed here, within peer group culture in London and other cities. Indeed, for these other groups of pupils in this report, our most significant learning, as researchers and teachers, is not to be represented by tables and distributions, but is carried in the texture of different conversations in different classrooms throughout the year. At the centre of the complexity introduced into London classrooms by the presence of overseas dialects of English, lies what we have called London/Jamaican — a magnetic, political, social and peer group dialect for Eastern as well as Western Caribbean pupils and to some extent for West African and even white London speakers too. The central point is that the range of different patois spoken reflects both the complexity of the linguistic situation in the Caribbean and also the modifications to these being made by children growing up within the overseas speech communities in London.

In the absence of more detailed study, the classification of possibilities among speakers of overseas dialects, with which we operated in administering the questionnaire, does no more than map diagrammatically the terrain. We have already discussed this more fully in Chapter 2 (pp. 29–36).

Within an overall distinction between Caribbean and non-Caribbean dialects of English, we asked our teachers to address their attention to three principal categories: (a) Standard, (b) a full regional Creole, or (c) a London/regional mix. Information about which patois, if any, was spoken was typically volunteered by the pupils themselves rather than detected linguistically. We are aware that all such information must be interpreted as indicative rather than hard and fast. In our view, it was better to err on the side of reflecting what are important cultural and linguistic distinctions, even if on occasion on slender evidence, than to promote a non-discriminating sense of West Indian patois or, more broadly, of overseas dialects.

As well as a general map of overseas dialects of English, we also sought through later questions to form some estimate of extent of use of patois, within a spectrum which stretches between pupils who are straightforwardly speakers of Great Britain based London or Standard and those (usually recent arrivals in this country) for whom patois is the dominant speech resource. A more delicate awareness of such differences would seem to have clear and important implications for our general educational understandings. As many teachers subsequently confirmed to us, there can be no ready asumption that all pupils 'of West Indian origin' are necessarily speakers of an overseas dialect of English nor that their speaking of a Great Britain based dialect of English is markedly distinct. On the other hand, it is just as important to avoid the corresponding stereotype that the speech of all West Indian pupils, because they are fluent talkers in London classrooms, is identical with that of Great Britain based London or Standard speakers. The much more subtle reality, different for each pupil, can only be resolved by listening to and talking with children. We report on such questions later.

Putting together in one breath all other overseas (non-Caribbean) dialects of English is a classifier's crudity only excused by the predictably smaller number of pupils to be included beneath such a heading. Here, and elsewhere, we need to register what is a research and not a cultural bias. Equally we offered no supporting classification to our teachers of these non-Caribbean, overseas dialects beyond a division between Standard or regional variant and a request to specify a name for dialect, country or area. Again we relied in practice for our information principally on what was told us by pupils. So the overall list of overseas dialects with which we emerged, as one outcome of the survey, includes references, for example, to American standard, West African pidgin and the like. We were tolerant of vagueness here and it represents a further line which might be followed up in greater detail.

To sum up then: the two way classification by country and type of dialect given in Table 8 rests on three simple categories:

1   *Speakers of a full Creole of the particular region*, sometimes, but by no means always a dominant speech resource.
2   *Speakers of Standard English*, but, broadly, a standard to be found in the particular region or a UK standard modified by the incorporation of some overseas features.
3   *Mixed London/other region* — speakers who incorporated lexis, syntax or idioms deriving from an overseas dialect (Creole) within their speech, but modified, usually heavily, by London English.

It is a limited first step, leaving a number of features either simply ambiguous or to be clarified by further evidence from the sample. For example, we shall go on to look at the questions about the strength of dialectal features in the speech of pupils

Table 8 Distributions for pupils speaking an overseas dialect of English by country of origin and type of dialect spoken

N = 711

	Creole (N = 100)	Standard (N = 70)	London/overseas dialect (N = 500)
Jamaica (N = 507)	52	11	444
Eastern Caribbean (N = 121)			
Antigua	6		3
Barbados	9	7	10
Dominica	3		5
Grenada	8	3	6
Guyana	2	1	12
Martinique			1
Montserrat			1
Nevis		1	
St Lucia	6	6	12
St Vincent	1		3
Trinidad	7	4	3
Tobago	1		
Africa (N = 30)			
Nigeria		15	
Uganda		2	
Ghana		4	
Mauritius		1	
South Africa		1	
'West Africa' (unidentified)	1		
Sierra Leone	4	2	
Other Countries (N = 12)			
USA		8	
Canada		1	
Australia		2	
New Zealand		1	

Miscellaneous attributions (e.g.) to Caribbean general not included = 41.

speaking an overseas dialect of English; and at the extent to which the overseas dialect is used. For Standard speakers, the table does not distinguish between pupils who are speakers of a full, overseas standard (e.g. from the Caribbean or West

Africa) and those who are speakers of a UK Standard, incorporating some overseas features. For all its limitations, however, Table 8 gives clear indications of range and major concentrations in type of dialect among the overseas dialect speakers in our sample.

Languages other than English

The final strand in the language diversity found in our twenty-eight schools seems to us, even now, breathtaking. We begin with Mouna as an example. Mouna's mother came from Pakistan. Mouna spoke to her in a Pakistani language (Gujerati) sometimes, but more usually she spoke Arabic, her father's first language. Her father spoke six languages. Mouna herself during her time in East Africa had begun to speak Swahili. Now in her east London school, she was forgetting this. Her spoken and written English were fluent, partly, Mouna said, as a result of her father's instruction before school, each morning. She still spoke Arabic well of course and thought of herself mainly as an Arabic speaker. But, unlike her brothers who had taken exams in Arabic, she was forgetting how to read and write it.

We give this one example to add some texture to the figure of 750 bilingual and multilingual pupils in our sample, constituting a proportion of 14 per cent. Mouna is typical of a smaller grouping within these in being actually plurilingual. One in sixty in our sample was, like Mouna, plurilingual, speaking two or more languages as well as English.

The repertoires of numbers of these children straddle the neatly classificatory boundary between speakers of an overseas dialect of English and speakers of a different overseas language other than English. Some West African children are, for example, both bidialectal and bilingual in their country of origin having in their repertoire English, standard and pidgin, and a tribal or local language. Or we might cite East African Asian children, for whom English has been in Kenya or Uganda, very much more than a hesitant, secondary resource. The examples could be multiplied. The majority of bilingual children were allocated, as we have already seen, as unambiguously speakers of English, on the basis of their classroom speech. In approaching possibilities such as these through our questionnaire, we wanted both to see bilingualism as one dimension within linguistic diversity in general and also to catch something of the various forms which it may take within the repertoires of different pupils.

For reasons already set out, we can make no cast iron estimate of the scale on which each of the languages listed in Table 9 is spoken through London as a whole. But our findings chime with everyday experience. European languages and South Asian languages predominate. A number of languages are spoken by groups of a substantial size, while there is also a wide variety of others commanding a few speakers here and there. For thirty-seven of the languages in our sample, the number of speakers was less than twelve. The remaining eighteen languages, by contrast account for 82 per cent of the bilingual population.

Within these major languages, well over half of the bilingual pupils in our sample were speakers of one of six European languages; the five South Asian languages constituting the other major grouping. Arabic, Cantonese, Yoruba and a range of French Creoles deriving from the West Indies and Mauritius were also spoken in substantial numbers. The high incidence of Greek and Turkish, given the bias in our sample, is not surprising. A probable under-representation is of South Asian languages, both in numbers of speakers and in actual languages represented. An example of such a language, for which we encountered no speakers, would be Tagalog, also spoken in the Philippines. A grouping, perhaps highlighted, is the number of West African languages, in particular Yoruba. We did not predict these being spoken on such a scale.

These lists of languages other than English formally complete the dimensions of language diversity in London schools. It is some effort of mind to return from such abstractions to in-dividual speakers of Greek, Turkish, Urdu, and Cantonese. It is also some effort of mind to hold the range of variety in some sort of unity in one's head. As we have said in Chapter 1, only a most ingenious model could incorporate the distribution of dialects and languages and their interaction. Here we have been concerned only with three dimensions. We have been drawing on the recording of repertoires of pupils, pupil by pupil, class by class, to attempt some sort of proportional answer to the question 'Who speaks what?' Only for the speakers of Great Britain based dialects of English have we passed beyond this to consider any sort of qualitative evidence as to the strength of features in the speech. For the bidialectal and bilingual speakers in our sample, similar qualitative evidence as to the strength of overseas dialectal features (for bidialectal pupils), extent of use of either dialect or language and literacy in

Table 9 Languages other than English, where spoken by one or more pupils

European	African	South Asian	Mid-Eastern	Far Eastern	Other
Greek	Yoruba	Gujerati	Iranian	Cantonese	French Creoles
Turkish	Hausa	Bengali	'Moroccan'	Chinese (new)	(Domincan, St Lucian,
Italian	Ibo	Punjabi	Arabic	standard	Guyanese, Mauritian)
Spanish	'Gambian'	Hindi		Mandarin	Maori
German	Gur	Urdu		Japanese	Maltese
Portuguese	Swahili	Katchi		Malay	Romany
French	Twi	Nepalese			
Dutch	Zulu	Pushtu			
Finnish	Afrikaans	Sinhalese			
Gaelic		Tamil			
Hungarian					
Polish					
Swedish					
Serbo-Croat					
Sloven					
Russian					
Armenian					
Latvian					
Yiddish					
Hebrew					
21	9	10	3	5	7

Total number of languages 55

63

dialect or overseas language was sought. That constituted a first step towards the more detailed studies which we hope will follow this report. It will also, we hope, increase the awareness of the bidialectal and bilingual repertoires possessed by only a little less than a third of the children in our sample.

5 THE RESULTS: HOW MUCH AND HOW OFTEN?

A richer picture of the numbers of dialects crowding London classrooms is a beginning in our study of language diversity. Plainly, though, a merely charted awareness of numbers and names is not enough. As we have indicated in Chapter 2, a full understanding raises very intricate questions indeed, in the study of which we are only at a beginning. At the least we need to know what is the strength and vitality of languages and dialects in the communities feeding schools and what is the availability of literacy in such languages and dialects for pupils growing up in these communities. The data give us some interesting indications of the answers. But at the heart of the matter lies detailed information about what is happening to different language communities as such communities put down new roots, adapt and change — information which is urgently needed and which we had no pretensions to having unearthed. The work of the Linguistic Minorities Project should make a major contribution, above all by providing sharpened sociolinguistic tools for investigators.

That such questions are relevant and important to the bilingual and bidialectal pupils in our sample was confirmed over and over again in our conversations with them. Seldom were they unclear about how much or how little they spoke the language indigenous among their people, about the attitudes of the adults nearest them towards such speaking or about their own feelings and concerns as speakers. There is no intention to suggest that all such pupils were fluent speakers of another language or dialect: some estimate of fluency was one direction of our questioning. But those who declared themselves uninterested in speaking an indigenous language or dialect did so, nearly always, against the background of a conscious set of expectations deriving from parents and families, whether for or against such an attitude. Those who declared themselves unable to speak more than a few words or phrases knew too

Table 10   Distribution of languages other than English, where
spoken by more than 14 pupils

	N	Percentage of bilingual pupils (N = 749) %
Greek	(165)	22
Turkish	(97)	13
Italian	(46)	6
Gujerati	(41)	5
Spanish	(35)	5
Cantonese	(33)	4
French Creoles	(33)	4
German	(30)	4
Portuguese	(28)	4
Bengali	(20)	3
Punjabi	(18)	2
French	(17)	2
Yoruba	(17)	2
Arabic	(16)	2
Hindi	(15)	2
Urdu	(15)	2

what they felt about this. The questions were important questions to them.

Overseas dialects of English and languages other than English clearly do not raise entirely the same sets of questions about the extent to which they are spoken or the availability of literacy within them. We treat them in this section both separately and in common, partly for reasons of economy in presentation. Our discussion, on the other hand, will attempt to treat the data appropriately. Language and dialect maintenance can at times share common territory. The possibilities for literacy in Caribbean Creoles would illustrate this common ground now that attitudes towards patois are changing both in the West Indies and here in Britain. We therefore need to keep dialect and language together for certain purposes.

Overseas dialects of English: bidialectal speakers
The range of dialects of English which we have loosely gathered under the heading overseas dialects, distinguished by a sub-population of bidialectal speakers, includes orders of marked

social, linguistic and cultural difference. That point needs to be made clear at the outset. The common category represents not a coherent unity, but a forced collection comprising dialects of very different status, different sociolinguistic bases both here and overseas and — arguably — very different prestige. So far we have made central in classifying this heterogeneity the general linguistic categories: full regional Creole, overseas standards, London/mixed. Such categories reflect important cultural differences in the phonology, lexis, syntax and idioms of pupils' speech. They are what we heard as teachers and researchers in allocating the speech of pupils as we talked to them. In approaching the question of how much and how often such overseas dialects were used by the pupils, we cannot simply leave the matter there. Differences such as these are sociolinguistic differences as much as structural ones and incorporate a history.

We can suggest a few pointers to the interpretation of change within the overlapping speech communities in London. Relative proportions are, as we have seen, strongly weighted. Pupils from the Caribbean dominate and within that group Jamaican, in particular, London/Jamaican dominates. A very much smaller proportion derive from the Eastern Caribbean and a proportion smaller still from different parts of Africa — especially from West Africa. Even so, pupils from Nigeria, speaking a modified Standard, when taken with Yoruba speakers (included as bilingual speakers), constitute a sub-population in our sample as large as the Cantonese or Spanish one. We need to know the linguistic and sociolinguistic history behind such groupings. We do not mean the migratory patterns but the patterns of language use which are generated over time.

In the meantime, it seems likely that social class, perhaps as much as the region of origin, must underlie the feature marked in Table 8: the contrast between regional and standard speakers. As that table indicates:

(i) most overseas dialect speakers outside the Caribbean were judged to be speakers of Standard

(ii) in contrast, the Jamaican sub-group contained only 2 per cent of speakers of Standard

(iii) speakers from the Eastern Caribbean were more polarized tending to speak either Creole or Standard

(iv) 87 per cent of the Jamaican group were allocated as

London/Jamaican speakers whereas the equivalent London/Caribbean mixture constituted 46 per cent of the Eastern Caribbean group.

We can go no further in our interpretation than to conjecture that these tendencies arise from social factors in the pattern of migration and that London/Jamaican speech in all its variety is a relatively independent entity attracting some pupils of Caribbean origin rather than others.

These suggestions, however, and their extension in a more general picture of bidialectal speakers in our sample are borne out by findings about how extensively the overseas dialect is used. This is a difficult question we are aware and evidence about it correspondingly difficult to assess. Attitudes towards an overseas dialect, particularly among West Indian communities, are very different from attitudes towards the mother tongue among speakers of languages other than English. Our questionnaire operated only with the broadest categories. The picture of Caribbean dialects, especially, which emerges in our findings is, however, typically that of a second or third generation. For few pupils is the overseas dialect dominant. Most are basically London speakers, who may occasionally deepen overseas dialectal features in certain contexts or for certain purposes. Yet relatively greater proportions of Jamaican (rather than Eastern Caribbean) pupils are estimated as regular dialect speakers; and the dialect regularly spoken, rather than full Jamaican Creole, is typically London/Jamaican. The relatively easier access to London/Jamaican speech would seem to be suggested by this. The figures are certainly compatible. The possibility, moreover, must accord with the experience of many teachers in London schools.

Against this background, it is not surprising that, among children who declared themselves interested in reading and writing material in an overseas dialect of English, Jamaicans similarly dominate. This is the point at which language and dialect should not be given separate consideration. Firstly, the response is affected by the availability in this country of printed material produced in the country of origin and, secondly, the extent to which materials are now being produced in the UK and, finally, how accessible either kind is to an individual pupil. Such material is by no means available to all languages; still less to different dialects. Given this fact, it is striking that as high

Table 11 Strength of overseas dialect features in the speech of bidialectal pupils (numbers in sample)

	Jamaican	Eastern Caribbean	Non-Caribbean Countries	Miscellaneous	TOTAL
A full overseas, dialectal speech	20	3	6		29
Basically a London (or Standard) speaker though incorporating some overseas dialectal features	487	118	36	41	682

Table 12 Extent of use of overseas dialect in the speech of bidialectal pupils (numbers in sample)

	Jamaican	Eastern Caribbean	Non-Caribbean	Miscellaneous	TOTAL
Speaks the overseas dialect regularly in certain contexts	90	8			98
Overseas dialect is pupil's dominant speech	17	4	8		29
Basically a London (or Standard) speaker, but occasionally deepens overseas dialectal features	400	109	34	41	572

Table 13	Interest in reading and writing in an overseas dialect among bidialectal pupils

	Percentages of bidialectal pupils %
Significantly interested in reading and writing in an overseas dialect	26
Not particularly interested in doing so	43
Opportunity is not realistically available within pupil's dialect	4
Not accurately described by any of the above	2
No information received in survey returns	25

a figure as 26 per cent were judged to be 'significantly interested' in reading and writing in an overseas dialect. Of these, by far the greater number are Jamaican. It would be valuable to know how far school policy exerts an influence on local bookshops and community activities.

To sum up then: the proportion of bidialectal pupils speaking an overseas dialect of English particularly, though not exclusively, comprises Caribbean speakers of one sort or another. It is a substantial sub-population. Many of these pupils are in the course of accommodating to a Great Britain based dialect of English and some indeed have effectively known no other. We have perhaps overstressed this. If so, it is as corrective to overemphasis in the other direction on gaps between Creole speech and Standard English. Most West Indian pupils in our sample were not full Creole speakers, for whom overseas dialects were dominant, although this was the case for a minority. Nor typically did such pupils switch at will between one fully autonomous dialect and another. What we have called code-sliding is a better descriptive metaphor. Such speech has its own complexity and its own strengths and weaknesses within the

Table 14 Interest in reading and writing in an overseas dialect among bidialectal pupils, by dialect sub-population (numbers in sample)

	Jamaican	Eastern Caribbean	Non-Caribbean	Miscellaneous	TOTAL
Significantly interested in reading and writing in an overseas dialect	162	11	2	5	180
Not particularly interested in doing so	215	61	20	11	307
Opportunity not available) Not accurately described) by above) Information not returned)	130	49	20	25	224

demands of secondary-school classrooms. Whatever the educational considerations to which the linguistic facts give rise, they cannot be based on assumptions of sharp discontinuities between British English and Caribbean English.

There are indications of a special role for Jamaican — London/Jamaican specifically. Pupils speaking London/Jamaican were more likely to be regular speakers of the dialect and more likely to be interested in Creole reading and writing. By the same token they were less likely than others to be Standard speakers. Much of this must be familiar to London teachers. It reinforces the need for an informed and refined view of the Caribbean Creole. Implicit in this is a further general point: that the questions and tables in our survey are entwined with descriptive, historical issues.

Difference according to gender (sex roles) and the impact of different schools on their Caribbean pupils are two further interesting strands on which we can offer a little evidence in our sample. Once again we can suggest an area well worth further study. The gender differences are not all one way. Girls were more likely to converge towards Standard and more likely to be allocated in Section A as unambiguously speakers of a Great Britain based dialect and less likely (but only a little) to be speakers of Caribbean patois. Those that were allocated as patois speakers, though, were more likely to be interested in reading and writing dialect material. Such indications have to be set against more general gender differences — a higher proportion of girls recorded as Standard speakers in our sample and a marked superiority, as estimated by teachers, in reading and writing.

It seems probable that regular speaking of patois and interest in reading and writing in it are in part fostered by schools and in part dependent on the support of a wider community. There are indications along these lines within our sample. On the one hand, readers and writers of an overseas dialect tend to be drawn from schools with a high population of overseas dialect speakers; but then that is hardly surprising since the majority of speakers of overseas dialects are contributed by these schools anyway. More significant is that within the nine or so schools with such substantial populations, interest in reading and writing in overseas dialect is much more marked in some schools rather than others. Such differences, like those of gender, are not to be weighted as of great importance here. They are indications of dimensions of which a full analysis would need to take account.

There is perhaps one dimension within a more detailed study which is of particular interest, namely the interconnectedness of Caribbean patois with other dialects of English in the London classroom. An understanding of the London component within London/Jamaican may be as important to fostering language and learning as an understanding of the Jamaican. For our pupils were not Jamaican pupils in London merely, but London Jamaicans. That is a gnomic and relatively crude formulation. It is a reminder of a consideration not addressed by our survey but central to any discussion of the speech of black pupils in London schools. That belongs with a full consideration of social class, language and education.

Bilingual speakers

Much of what has been written so far about the need for interpretation applies equally in considering the bilingual speakers in our sample. Such a heading covers, as we have seen, an enormous range of different languages, some comprising relatively substantial numbers of speakers, others much more thinly spread. Clearly not all pupils loosely described as bilingual up to this point were equally fluent both in English and another language. But many were. Roughly half the children speaking a language other than English were allocated as 'effectively bilingual' and speaking an overseas language regularly in certain contexts; the other half was composed of smaller proportions having 'the overseas language dominant' or alternatively as having 'only a good understanding' or 'speaking not more than a few words and phrases'. Half these pupils, in addition, had some facility in reading and writing in the overseas language.

That is *prima facie* evidence, then, of substantial numbers of bilingual and biliterate pupils, whose resources and competences in language have traditionally received very little positive recognition in schools. Yet our understanding, as for bidialectal pupils, needs to go deeper. Differences between the major languages listed in Table 15 in the degree to which the mother tongue is maintained can be derived, all reservations as to size of sample entered, from figures on the *extent* to which the language is used by the relevant speakers in our sample. Such figures offer no more than the beginnings of a framework; and a few speculations are therefore in order. Viewed as a whole, it is more common for speakers of South Asian languages, or of Arabic or Cantonese to be bilingual speakers (or to have the overseas language dominant) than for European speakers — a point which might be extended a number of ways. Similarly, within the South Asian languages it is the local Gujerati, Punjabi and Bengali which are available to bilingual speakers rather than the national Hindi and Urdu. Among European languages, figures for French and German reflect presumably the absence of communities settled in the UK in which these languages might be a daily resource outside as well as within the home. For these as for other speakers we may also suppose a different kind of underlying history and social composition. Explanations of this sort are also needed for the relatively small proportions of bilinguals among speakers of French Creoles or Yoruba. Indications such as these are no more than tantalizing and speculative glimpses of possible distinctions. We need to catch up with some other countries on our understanding of bilingualism and when we do, it will most certainly emerge that there are features peculiar to Britain as well as ones which we share.

A further step is needed. We can suggest profiles for the sub-groups speaking different languages, if one or two further dimensions of data are added to the picture reflected in Table 15. Proportions of sub-groups of pupils reading and writing in the overseas language is one such dimension; also allocation on the basis of classroom speech and level of competence as a speaker of English.

One grouping to be made is of those languages with a relatively high proportion of speakers for whom they were the dominant language resource: Cantonese, Bengali, Arabic and Urdu. These were the dominant languages for over a quarter of the pupils who spoke them, as shown in Table 15. Relatively few speakers of these languages were allocated as unambiguously speakers of English (on average 30 per cent and as low as 18 per cent for speakers of Cantonese); and relatively high proportions, correspondingly, were allocated in the initial or intermediate stage of competence as speakers of English. We took no record in our sample of duration of stay in the United Kingdom. Relatively recent arrival may be one explanation for this pattern. There are no doubt others. In our sample, at any rate, it is for speakers of these languages that questions of provision for English as a second language appear most appropriate. And to these four languages we may also add speakers of Gujerati, differentiated by a smaller proportion for whom the overseas language was dominant and, correspondingly, a larger proportion who were effectively bilingual. A final point concerns literacy in the language other than English. This was estimated as high for speakers of Cantonese. Bengali, Arabic and Urdu but relatively low for speakers of Gujerati (also, as we shall see, for speakers of Punjabi and Hindi).

Speakers of Hindi, French, Italian, Yoruba, French Creoles and German constitute a grouping at the opposite pole. Here the incidence of bilingualism or language dominance is substantially lower; and larger proportions of speakers of these languages were estimated either as having good understanding, but speaking only a little or as speaking no more than a few words and phrases. The proportions can be noted from the 'other' column in Table 15. Large numbers of these speakers also were allocated as unambiguously speakers of English on the basis of their classroom speech. Finally, literacy in the overseas language is also contrastive with the other grouping. For speakers of French the incidence is relatively high. For speakers of Hindi, Italian, Yoruba and various French Creoles, it is less than 25 per cent.

The remaining European languages, Greek and Turkish, Portuguese and Spanish are less clearly marked as a grouping. Together with Punjabi, approximately half the speakers of these languages were allocated as unambiguously English speakers (in Greek as high as 72 per cent) — a high proportion, certainly, but markedly lower than for the French and Italian speakers and for the second grouping generally. Like the second grouping though, only a small proportion of speakers of these languages was estimated as in the initial or intermediate stages of learning English; though a higher proportion was allocated as bilingual.

There is no need to go further. The intention behind this loose classification is partly to organize a range of data, but also to do some justice by questions on which there is some indicative evidence in our sample, slight though it is. Educational and other provision (the school and local library, for example) needs to take some account of the degree to which mother tongue and literacy in mother tongue is being maintained, not merely overall, but in separate language communities. Our guess is that our figures would be compatible with an interpretation of gradual assimilation of different linguistic communities,

Table 15   Comparison of amount of use of languages other than English, where spoken by more than fourteen pupils

Percentages of sub-groups speaking each language

	Bilingual: regularly speaks language %	Overseas language dominant %	Other: speaks some phrases %
Gujerati	80	10	10
Punjabi	66	17	17
Greek	65	5	30
Turkish	61	0.2	39
Cantonese	60	27	13
Bengali	60	30	10
Arabic	56	25	19
Portuguese	54	14	32
Spanish	51	14	35
Hindi	53	—	47
French Creoles	39	3	57
Italian	39	2	59
French	35	—	65
Urdu	33	27	40
German	23	—	77
Yoruba	23	—	77

except where strong cultural interest or substantial language communities (Greek, for example) serve to maintain them. It is necessary to check on interpretation of figures for the bilingual population as a whole to have some idea of the strands which compose them. Tables by the major overseas languages for allocation as unambiguously a speaker of English, for literacy in the overseas language and for competence as a speaker of English are set out on pages 76–7.

6   THE RESULTS: GENDER DIFFERENCES

So far then we have tried to provide some answers to the two questions: 'Who speaks what?' and 'How much and how often?' Our findings have indicated a wide range of dialects and languages. We have looked at a spectrum of Great Britain based dialects of English, and those features more strongly marked

Table 16   Comparisons of proportions of pupils allocated as
'Unambiguously speakers of English' or as 'Incorporating features
deriving from a language other than English' for languages, where spoken
by more than fourteen pupils

	Percentages of sub-groups speaking each language	
	Unambiguously speakers of English %	Incorporating features from overseas language %
German	90	10
Yoruba	88	12
Italian	82	18
French	82	18
Hindi	73	27
Greek	72	28
French Creoles	60	40
Turkish	60	40
Spanish	60	40
Portuguese	50	50
Punjabi	50	50
Gujerati	41	59
Urdu	40	60
Arabic	31	69
Bengali	30	70
Cantonese	18	82

Table 17   Proportions of pupils estimated as reading and writing in a
language other than English, where spoken by more than fourteen pupils

	Percentages of sub-groups speaking each language	
	Reads and writes %	Reads but does not write %
Cantonese	64	12
Spanish	66	6
Bengali	30	31
Urdu	40	20
French	53	6
Arabic	50	6
Portuguese	43	11
Turkish	42	12
Greek	37	16
German	37	7
Gujerati	24	12
Hindi	13	23
Italian	21	4
Punjabi	17	5
Yoruba	11	11
French Creoles	3	18

Table 18   Estimates of competence as speakers of English for pupils speaking a language other than English, where spoken by more than fourteen pupils

Percentages of sub-groups speaking each language

	Initial %	Intermediate %	Fluent %
Cantonese	18	36	46
Bengali	15	35	50
Arabic	25	12	63
Urdu	13	13	74
Gujerati	5	15	80
Portuguese	6	14	80
Spanish	11	6	83
Hindi		13	87
Greek		12	88
Turkish	1	11	88
French		12	88
Punjabi	5	5	90
French Creoles		9	91
Italian		9	91
Yoruba		6	94
German		3	97

for some pupils than others. We have seen that among the first-year pupils in our twenty-eight schools, large numbers were either bidialectal or bilingual. We have tried to make some qualitative estimate of this. In the closing sections of this report we raise some further questions. We shall not be explicitly concerned with implications for teachers and schools of linguistic diversity, at this point. That is for our next chapter to ponder. But the questions which we shall be raising now are best seen with notions of policy and practical teaching in mind. Assuming such an orientation towards classroom and school, we shall be adding now some comment on what else it might be helpful to know.

In earlier sections we have mostly been concerned with differences between different language groupings based on appropriate sub-populations in the sample. In presenting such findings, we have taken no account of differences between boys and girls in such matters as the strength of features in dialectal speech, tendency towards Standard English, maintenance of or interest in an overseas dialect or language. It seemed reasonable to suppose that general findings on these questions would serve as a first step in engaging with complex questions. Yet differences by gender within these broad patterns of findings might have important implications: important to our overall understanding of ways in which language is used in society, findings about such differences could also further help approaching language diversity in the classroom.

Table 19   Comparison of boys and girls by main language groupings
(excluding considerations of bidialectalism and bilingualism)

	Boys %	Girls %
Great Britain based dialects of English		
London	65	69
Non-London Regional	2	2
Standard	14	16
Overseas based dialects of English	12	9
Languages other than English	7	4

Table 20   Gender by strength of dialectal features in Great Britain based dialects of English

	Boys %	Girls %
Full London	34	31
Weak London	31	38
Weak Standard	9	9
Strong Standard	5	7

Approaching gender differences from within our data is a relatively simple matter. Since the sex of each pupil was recorded as part of the initial identifying information, all that is involved is dividing the data in two. That is relatively easily done. Nor is it difficult then to cross-tabulate boys and girls with all the data which we have so far considered independently. We give such details of procedure, not out of concern for minutiae, but as a warning, that issue of relationships gender and language is too complex to be encompassed by the variables in our data. Nonetheless, here too we unearthed some facts which can contribute to the debate.

Almost a tradition in the study of language and gender by now (Labov, 1972a; Trudgill, 1974) is the tendency for girls to be more likely to be speakers of Standard and for boys to be stronger dialect speakers. Our sample is no exception. Things are not absolutely as straightforward as that implies, since a rather greater proportion of girls than boys, who spoke a Great Britain based dialect of English, were allocated as London speakers. Against this apparently contradictory evidence, we have to set two further considerations. Firstly, differences in strength of dialectal features within the groupings for London and Standard. Girls, more likely than boys to be speakers of Standard, were also more likely to be speakers of a full Standard rather than one converging on London speech. Boys, though a smaller proportion of them were allocated as London speakers, were appreciably more likely to use a full London speech and less likely to converge on Standard. Differences in the figures are not great. The relatively small size of the difference is perhaps as important a finding. But the tendency is unmistakable.

A second consideration explains the apparently contradictory finding of a larger proportion of girls than boys allocated as London speakers. This is that an appreciably larger proportion of girls than boys was allocated to Section A of the questionnaire (as unambiguously speakers of a Great Britain based dialect of English) rather than to Section B (incorporating features deriving from an overseas language or dialect). While this partly explains the higher proportion allocated to London, it also raises new issues. On the one hand, the figures suggest that boys speaking an overseas (e.g. Caribbean) dialect of English were more likely to retain features from such a dialect in their speech and girls correspondingly to modify them more radically. That would be in accordance with the general tendency towards Standard indicated so far. On the other hand, it is also the case that substantially more boys than girls in our sample spoke either an overseas dialect or a language other than English.

Table 21 Bilingual and bidialectal speakers —
Comparison of boys and girls

	Boys %	Girls %
Speaks an overseas dialect, but classroom speech reflects no features from it	4	5
Speaks a language other than English, but classroom speech reflects no features from it	10	10
Speaks an overseas dialect and features from it are reflected in classroom speech	12	9
Speaks a language other than English and features from it are reflected in classroom speech	7	4
Total bidialectal	16	14
Total bilingual	17	14

Table 22 Estimates of competence in reading and writing standard English
— Comparison of boys and girls

	Boys %	Girls %
Reading		
Fluent	43	49
Intermediate	39	36
With difficulties	18	15
Writing		
Fluent	33	40
Intermediate	43	41
With difficulties	24	19

The further main tendency in the differences by gender, if tendency rather than accident it is, is for boys to retain overseas languages and dialects and for girls to be monolingual speakers. We can only confess that we ourselves were puzzled by this discrepancy. One possible explanation is that a general tendency across the range of different cultural groupings represented in our sample is for pressures to be on boys rather than girls to maintain mother tongues or not to jettison overseas dialect. But this would be surprising. We need to distinguish here between different attitudes within families and minority groups towards mother tongue, as opposed to such attitudes towards dialect. The impression which we had formed through the year was that whereas girls might be more likely to accommodate their speech through doubts about dialect, they were correspondingly more likely, from family pressure, to maintain mother tongue. Certainly there is no support for this hypothesis within our data. But in the end, we doubt whether there is a contrasting hypothesis to be mounted about boys, as one interpretation of our findings might suggest. It seems more likely that our sample was in this respect simply unbalanced. Our data give us information about numbers of pupils speaking an overseas language or dialect. They do not give us information about numbers of pupils, allocated in Section A, who *might* have had access to a language other than English but have not maintained it. Such data would be necessary to resolve the question.

Paradoxically it might seem, in view of their fewer numbers, it is girls rather than boys who show more interest in reading and writing in a language other than English and in an overseas dialect. This brings us to the second clear finding (the first is the girls' tendency towards Standard) about gender and language diversity in our sample. Not only were more girls estimated by teachers as highly fluent readers and writers, but also consistently fewer were estimated as having significant difficulties. We shall deal more generally with literacy in the next section. Here we may merely comment that there seemed to be a general tendency within the sample for pupils to be estimated as reading better than they wrote and girls scored markedly better as both writers and readers. But this is also a relatively hallowed finding in the literature and needs no further comment.

Analysis of differences by gender within the complex, linguistic interaction of London classrooms seems to us an important research area. Since, within perhaps certain very general tendencies, such differences are likely to be differently mediated within different cultures, a most intricate analysis is needed. If this area could be more fully explored, a significant new perspective would be given to an area of study which has only recently been opened up.

7 THE RESULTS: READING AND WRITING

Reading and writing represent the next extension on which we gathered some evidence in our investigation.

Written language

Teachers will need no reminding that conflicting assumptions and beliefs lie at the heart of any discussion of school, literacy and children. Recognition of school achievements is hard to win; and every sympathetic discussion tends to assume common norms of pupil achievement with this or that group disadvantaged from that norm. Several years after Bullock's flat assertion that no single measure currently developed could ever monitor adequately the range of activities, processes and attitudes which constitute reading in school, simplistic correlations between groups of pupils and tested scores are not uncommon. Distinctions between statistical significance and educational significance, which always needs profound, conceptual interpretation are rarely observed. It is not our intention here to add to or support such studies.

As one extension to our work, however, interaction between speech and written language in classroom situations of multiple diversity seems to us an important area of study. Typically such interaction has been approached hitherto either from relatively general, usually psycholinguistic, perspectives or from the vantage of one or other minority group (E2L learners, West Indian children, social class differences). What is needed, we submit, is an approach which begins from the differently ordered complexities of actual classrooms and which studies the interaction of spoken and written language within the rhythms, alliances, expectations and attitudes of classroom process. This, after all, is the complexity confronting teachers.

The overall parameters of language diversity represented in our sample, together with indications about the extent to which dialects and languages are used, represents a very first sketch of the ecology for such a study. Within that, we also gathered through our questionnaire some coarse information more directly concerned with literacy. We have already touched one part of this — mother tongue literacy among bilingual pupils and interest in reading and writing in overseas dialects among bidialectals. We have also noted some indications of differences in such biliteracy in different language groupings. A second part to such information derives from estimates which we asked teachers to give of the fluency and independence of pupils as readers and writers within normal classroom learning. We asked for allocation of pupils to one of three categories (full definition of these can be seen in the questionnaire, (Appendix 2):

1   fluent and independent
2   intermediate
3   having significant difficulty.

Separate estimates were made of each pupil for reading and writing. Such estimates were intentionally left to be formed on the basis of teachers' general impressions and no attempt was made to standardize different teachers' judgments either within or across schools. As will be clear from this description of our procedure, we were concerned not to miss the opportunity of gathering some supplementary information which might

Table 23   Estimates of competence in reading and writing Standard English — General proportions

	%
Reading	
Fluent	46
Intermediate	37
With difficulties	17
Writing	
Fluent	37
Intermediate	42
With difficulties	21

suggest further lines of investigation rather than to develop a systematic account. It will also be clear, such data offers no objective basis for considerations of achievement, either by pupil or school, and was not intended as such.

Table 24 Reading and writing related to % of sub-group estimated as having significant difficulties in different language groupings

		Reading %	Writing %
1	Strong Standard (N= 267)	4	5
2	Weak Standard (N = 441)	6	9
3	Other countries overseas dialect, mainly Standards (N = 35)	11	11
4	Weak London (N = 1625)	15	19
5	London/Jamaican (N = 298)	15	21
6	Non-London: Great Britain based (N = 83)	17	24
7	East Caribbean (total) (N = 77)	19	30
8	Strong London (N = 1445)	22	27
9	Language other than English (N = 256)	29	35
10	Caribbean Creole speakers (N = 27)	37	37

Table 25 Estimates of competence in reading and writing standard English – bidialectal and bilingual pupils: row percentages

	Reading			Writing		
	1	2	3	1	2	3
Speaks an overseas dialect but classroom speech reflects no features from it	40	43	17	29	49	22
Speaks an overseas dialect and features from it are reflected in classroom speech	41	42	17	33	45	22
Speaks a language other than English but classroom speech reflects no features from it	50	35	15	42	41	17
Speaks a language other than English and features from it are reflected in classroom speech	25	46	29	19	46	35
Speaks a full, Caribbean Creole as dominant language	30	33	37	26	37	37

Table 26   Literacy in an overseas dialect or language and literacy in Standard English – Comparative cross-tabulation for those pupils for whom information is available

	Reading			Writing			N =
	1	2	3	1	2	3	
Speaks an overseas dialect of English							
Interested in writing in it	43	41	16	33	47	20	116
Not interested in writing in it	36	46	18	27	46	27	186
Speaks a language other than English							
Reads and writes in it	24	44	32	19	41	40	104
Reads only in it	23	53	24	14	54	32	66
Not literate in it	42	25	33	17	50	33	12

In the sample as a whole, the first and most general consideration is the discrepancy already touched between estimates for
reading and writing. On the whole, the tendency for estimates,
of literacy are unsurprising. A proportion of around 40 per cent
across schools were allocated to category (1), fluent and
independent, a further 40 per cent to category (2), intermediate, and 20 per cent to category (3), having significant
difficulties. There was no evidence returned by the teachers in
our sample, it should be said, of major difficulties with literacy
experienced by large numbers of pupils. The discrepancy
between reading and writing is, however, unmistakable and
since it is based on the total population in the sample is
supported by fairly considerable evidence. The discrepancy is
marked at both ends of the three point scale with which we
are operating. Pupils were less likely to be allocated as fluent
writers than readers (the difference is 9 per cent) and more
likely to be allocated as having significant difficulty in writing
(by 4 per cent). As we have seen, girls are more favourably
estimated than boys, both as readers and writers. But the
general discrepancy is marked for them as well. Nor is any
language grouping an exception to this.

Difference between estimates for reading and writing of
this kind reflects, presumably, the relatively greater difficulty
of production over reception, an old theme in linguistic literature; and marks what must be a relatively common experience
among London teachers. What we need, though, is to understand
such relatively greater difficulty as it is experienced within
the different language repertoires represented in our sample.
We may stress two aspects to such an understanding. We need
to consider in concrete terms the interaction between reading,
the production of written language and Standard speech as they
are mediated in the classroom. We also need to understand more
fully the resources within different speech repertoires from
which written language may be approached.

Teachers' estimates for fluency by different language groupings constitute one indicative step towards such a study. Three
very general observations serve to summarize the data:

1   There is an unmistakable tendency for Standard speakers
     to be estimated much more highly as readers and writers.
2   There is no evidence to suggest that bidialectal or bilingual
     pupils are in general markedly less fluent than their mono-

lingual (though not their Standard speaking) counterparts.

3   There is some not unexpected evidence to suggest that pupils who are still in initial or intermediate stages in learning English as a second language for whom an overseas based Creole is a dominant language are likely to be experiencing difficulties with reading and writing.

Such evidence is unremarkable enough if viewed merely as some kind of comment on standards. Taken with other evidence in the sample about language diversity it represents a pointer in the direction of further study.

As will be seen from Table 24, Standard speakers are clearly marked off from other language groupings. Not only were far fewer speakers of Standard (proportionally) felt to be experiencing difficulties with reading and writing (approximately 6 per cent), but very substantially higher proportions were allocated to category (1), fluent and independent. For speakers of a full Standard the figure is as high as 81 per cent. This figure serves, however, to introduce a more specific comment. The discrepancy of Standard speakers would be compatible with general explanatory theories of education and social class; and indeed this may well be what such a finding represents. What is further marked in our findings, however, are continua away from Standard, as one pole, towards London or overseas dialectal speech, which also correlates with estimates for reading and writing. Thus, pupils who were Standard speakers converging on London speech tended to be estimated less highly than speakers of full Standard, for example; and full London speakers less highly again than those London speakers for whom dialectal features are less marked. Analogously, speakers of overseas standards tended to be estimated more highly than London or vernacular speaking counterparts. There is even some tendency for speakers of Great Britain based dialects of English to be less highly estimated, the more their speech approaches London, rather than non-London regional speech.

Figures for bidialectal and bilingual speakers specifically need little additional comment. What they chiefly suggest is the need for careful discrimination in advancing theories in such matters. Not surprisingly, the proportions of bilingual pupils allocated to Section B (features of an overseas language reflected in classroom speech), who included in their number some pupils in initial and intermediate stages as speakers of English, tended to be less highly estimated as readers and writers in English. As important, in contrast, bilingual speakers allocated to Section A are estimated no differently from any other grouping save Standard. Such figures, we may suppose, are simply compatible with greater experience in English, while it remains true that a substantial minority of bilingual speakers are still experiencing difficulties. For bidialectal speakers, on the other hand, there is no marked difference in estimates between pupils allocated to Section A or Section B. Not surprisingly, however, a small minority of pupils for whom overseas Creole was reckoned as dominant tended also to be more likely to be experiencing significant difficulty. It should be stressed, however, that for by no means all Creole speakers was this the case.

One further matter on which we had hoped to gather some evidence was on the interaction between literacy in an overseas language and literacy in English. There is no need to spell out the importance of this for the kind of investigation which we have been sketching. As a simple exercise in correlation, however, this evidence is rendered inconclusive by our inability within our data to hold level of competence in English for the purposes of comparison. Greater numbers of pupils who are at the initial and intermediate stages of learning English as a second language tend also to compose the sub-population of those identified as writing and reading regularly in a language other than English. There is no such difficulty for bidialectal pupils who declared an interest in reading and writing in an overseas dialect. Our data here are very limited. Nevertheless, such pupils tend to be estimated more highly as readers and writers by our teachers. Such evidence would be compatible with the view that fostering literacy in general is better than a narrowly focused concentration on the target. On the other hand, they may be a special group marked by characteristics we could not ascertain. It is much too slender as evidence to be offered in conclusive support of any interpretation. But it does suggest that we ought to find out.

8   SCHOOLS AND THEIR DIFFERENCES

We spent a good deal of time in schools in the course of our investigation and most of that time we had the impression that they worked well. It is a relief to stress the pleasures of the enterprise. Intermediate meetings, introductory hurdles past, were spent comparing interim findings for different classes, talking about different children. Follow-up meetings, with the results for the school tabulated, were spent in discussion about findings and their implications. It was rare for there not to be some wrinkle or some unexpected result. The experience breeds the conviction which was deepened through the year that schools do need to look at their populations in ways similar to the ones which we had embarked upon. The systematization is itself a learning process generating new awareness and not unusually some new discoveries. Undertaken collaboratively by groups of staff, some such investigation can be a way of pooling insight.

Schools differ. One of the points which the overall process of conducting the survey seemed to lead to was a sense amongst teachers of the unique and specific nature of their own school population. It is actually rare for staff in a school to be able to place their experience against other schools' experiences. A systematic look at the languages and dialects present in the pupil population (staff as well were recurrently suggested) can light up an aspect of that experience for comparison.

Differences between schools in our survey reflect the principal directions of our investigation. Differences in language groups represented, stronger or weaker London speakers and more or less of them, more or less speakers of Caribbean or West African or other overseas dialects, spoken more or less extensively, different languages other than English, different degrees of bilingualism, bidialectalism and biliteracy, many or few or no children in initial stages of learning English as a second language, different levels of fluency and independence in reading and writing — all of these are relevant considerations. Just as important, all of these are experienced in school in some kind of total mix and not in separate dimensions which analysis neatly disposes.

Presentation of case sheet data on all such variables would be a wearisome business and need not detain us here. For the twenty-eight schools in our sample we need only to draw lines indicative of fundamental differences in the tasks that some rather than others were facing. Within that somewhat accidental collection of twenty-eight schools, 14 per cent only of ILEA schools, in different parts of London, linguistic composition was indeed very different. To take some indicative extremes, in one school no fewer than 98 per cent of the children were allocated as London speakers and all but 2 per cent of those as speaking a full London dialect; while in another at the opposite end of one spectrum the figure for London speakers is as low as 30 per cent, but a further 55 per cent of pupils were allocated as Standard. Nine of our schools, to take a different point of entry, possessed proportions of speakers of overseas dialect, mainly Caribbean, of over 27 per cent — as high as 47 per cent in one; while for fourteen schools the equivalent figure is 5 per cent or less. We counted twenty-eight different languages other than English in one school within a proportion of 22 per cent bilingual children. Elsewhere the proportion of bilingual children, if not of numbers of languages, was even higher. In three schools the proportion of bilinguals was over 30 per cent and in nine over 20 per cent. We return with more detail later to this subject when we argue the implications of such a range of difference for tailor-made school policy. Here we may note simply that the scale and range of differences is great.

Whether schools also make a difference is an important speculation. We have noted earlier some indication that interest in literacy in an overseas dialect is determined not merely by size of supporting population but also by school. It would be surprising if schools did not make some difference in this respect. We have undertaken no separate analysis though of difference in respect of extent to which overseas dialects are used or languages other than English maintained. On our data it does not seem that it would be very profitable to do so.

An outer London borough
Our sample was drawn, as we have explained, from two sources: from twenty-three schools within the ILEA, from five schools within one outer London borough, Haringey. We have taken no account of differences between these two sources in our general interpretation of the survey's findings, preferring, for our purposes, to talk simply of London schools.

Differences between the two areas, though present, are not sufficient to distort, in any marked fashion, our findings overall. For example, neither area has such a marked predominance in one language grouping that the equivalent general sub-total is substantially the effect of a sectional contribution. Nor are scorings on any particular qualitative scale such as to lead one

Table 27:   Differences between schools in main language groups

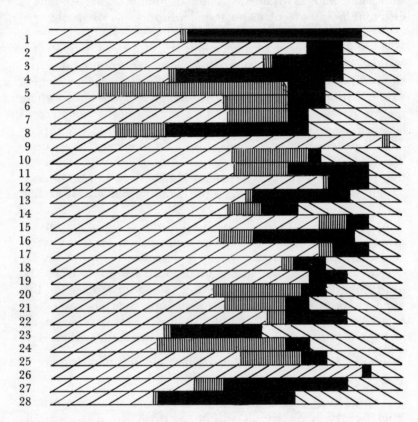

%
School Population

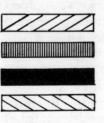

KEY

London

Standard

Bidialectal

Bilingual

92

to suppose local differences between ILEA and the Borough of Haringey to be greater than those between any two boroughs in the ILEA itself. It would be surprising if differences of this sort obtained. Common sense and experience suggest that language diversity is generally characteristic of London as a whole and that local differences are more complexly determined than on borough/ILEA lines.

The size of the Haringey sub-population is approximately 19 per cent of the total sample, that of the ILEA, correspondingly 81 per cent. Haringey contributes more than its proportional share to some of the major language groupings, and less to some others, but the differences are not massive. Respective shares of major language groupings are set out in Table 28.

Table 28   Composition of major language groupings — respective contributions from ILEA and Haringey

	ILEA (N = 3918) %	Haringey (N = 899) %	Total
London	57	10	67
Non-London	2	—	2
Standard	11	4	15
Overseas dialect	7	3	10
Other language	4	2	6

Differences between the Borough of Haringey's five schools and the twenty-one sampled in the ILEA are displayed in Table 29.

Table 29   Comparison of ILEA and Haringey — proportions in major language groupings

	ILEA %	Haringey %
London	71	51
Non-London	2	—
Standard	14	21
Overseas dialect	8	18
Other language	5	10

But our principal reflection is that too much should not be made of these. Certainly, differences in incidence of London,

Standard speech and of overseas dialects are clearly marked. But the implications of this would seem best incorporated in a more general reflection. Language diversity is powerfully and continuously present throughout London schools, displaying also differences, colossal at times, between area and area, between school and school. The differences between the ILEA and Haringey, while not distorting the findings overall, are essentially reminders of these local variations.

What we have sought to do in these last sections is to raise a number of further questions and extensions against the background of our main study. But we have left unaddressed so far the most important question of all, namely the implications of language diversity for the school setting and for policy more generally. To this question we devote the next chapter explicitly.

Much of the time we spent in school we spent with teachers talking to children about language. Parameters and tables and statistics are one end-product of such talking, as is the way of these things. But it is the conversation which stays in the head. That seems not unfitting.

Chapter 4　The implications of linguistic diversity

1　LANGUAGE DIVERSITY AND EDUCATION

> I think all of this is very interesting. I think you have succeeded in making me culturally aware. I am very sympathetic with the plight of the Mexican American and feel no prejudice against him. However, as a teacher, I want to know what to do *differently* for the Mexican American child from what I do for the Anglo child when I am teaching $2 + 2 = 4$. (Angel cited in Spolsky, 1972)

Multi-cultural education has struggled its way on to our national educational agenda. There were people of foresight and commitment fifteen to twenty years ago, and there have been others since who saw the wider implications of cultural and linguistic diversity but their impact, measured against need, has been relatively restricted. We do not mean that there have not been resources allocated to the education of particular minority groups and we have no intention of slighting the centres and teachers who have been at work, particularly in the field of teaching English as a second language. We mean rather that as distinct from specific language provision, it is only recently that we have come to realize that the whole curriculum for all children must change in the light of cultural diversity and that language diversity implies much more than teaching English to those who do not speak it. There may be the feeling that things are better now. We can point to many initiatives which show this to be so, but compared with what still needs to be done, we are confident that we are at a very early stage of the process which could make major changes in what happens in classrooms and in all those experiences which substantially affect children as learners.

Many, perhaps most of the efforts being made at this moment are relatively isolated from each other, are highly dependent on local enthusiasm and commitment and take on a particular emphasis, often through the specific skills and enthusiasm of individuals. These efforts are often made in the teeth of indifference, misunderstanding or even hostility. What has been lacking is a general strategy, a move across the whole front. One school will have an excellent ESL programme; and another will have initiated some effective mother tongue programmes; another will have experimented successfully with new examinations; another will have revised key areas of its curriculum. Some authorities have well-established centres, programmes and specialist advisers and teachers. But in very many classrooms teachers are still struggling with circumstances which baffle them.

Our assessment is that we have come through a period in which the broad lines of alternative policies have been sketched out. There is no shortage of statements, manifestos and guidelines. Needless to say, this does not mean that there has been a comfortable consensus. On the contrary, most of the issues we discuss in this chapter rapidly raise the heat of controversy. But that is the *level* at which the debate is conducted. Because experience has been so sparse, because we cannot draw upon a reservoir of well-attested and disseminated practice, we desperately lack that healthy corrective to statements of principle and intent, the experience of classroom teachers. It is a familiar stage of innovation and change, charged with nervousness, tentativeness and trial-and-error method. The writers of this report have no miraculous immunity from these difficulties.

We might have rested content with unearthing the statistics and left to others the implications which might be read from them.*

This would have been an abdication which was not to our taste. The teachers we have worked with and are working with would have been shocked by such timidity. In the hours we have spent with them in discussion, we returned again and again to *the educational meaning* of the figures. It was to this meaning we addressed ourselves in a conference we called while this report was in preparation (see Conference Report *Language*

*The most thorough and wide-scale language survey ever undertaken is probably *The Survey of Language Use and Teaching in East Africa*. Two of the leading participants comment '... expatriate team members have very serious reservations as to the wisdom and ethics of expressing their opinion on controversial issues...' (Ohannessian and Anste in Ohannessian *et al*, p. 155). Our investigation, a pygmy by comparison, was not carried out by expatriates and therefore was not inhibited by their reservations.

Diversity: the Implications for Policy and the Curriculum, Institute of Education, 1979). Our future work is planned to focus on this exploration.

2 DIVERSITY

Our figures are an indication of the massive change which has altered the linguistic profile of the schools in a very short space of time. It is without precedent in the history of compulsory schooling. Other countries are undergoing a similar experience and there are indications that they have gone further than us in response to it. (In Australia, for example, which comes closer to our pattern than many European countries. See for example Claydon *et al*, 1977 and the Parliament of the Commonwealth of Australia, 1975.)

It does not require any kind of survey to make people, especially teachers, aware of the language variety in schools. However, the precise nature of the variety was something of a surprise. One important and well-intentioned scheme of mother tongue teaching was actually launched in a provincial town and only after its inception was it discovered that their guesses on numbers were wildly out. Out of sheer necessity, many teachers lumped together Asian languages or something they called 'West Indian'. Moreover, the survey brought to light the hidden language resources of many pupils. The second language learner with obvious foreignness in speech obtrudes but the pupil who has native-like mastery of English may never give an indication that he is a speaker of another language, particularly if he believes that in some way it does not count. The survey, then, can bring home both quantitatively and qualitatively the multilingualism of our schools. In doing so, it should also bring out the need to take our study much further than it was able to go. There is no reason why schools should not carry out their own surveys for their whole population using our questionnaire in a modified form and enriching it with the kind of detail we could not afford to collect. We would stress that carrying out such work is in itself an educative process which changes the perceptions and sensitivities of the participants.

The fifty-five languages and twenty-four overseas-based dialects is an impressive array. It is widely accepted that the experience of the pupil must dovetail into the experience offered by school and that teachers have an obligation to understand that experience. Language is a central part of that experience and we are under no less an obligation, therefore, to undertake our education in linguistic diversity. We are not being Utopian. We do not believe that anyone can aspire to an encyclopaedic perfectionism. With the help of pupils and parents we could all learn much that would help us in our teaching. Above all, knowing more about the languages and dialects of the pupils would reduce the tendency to treat their education as 'remedial' or 'compensatory'.

It is not simply a matter of discovering a few useful facts about this or that language but also of developing an understanding of such slippery terms as 'bidialectal' or 'bilingual' which we discussed in Chapter 2. We may say of a speaker, to take the most difficult example, that he has in his repertoire both London English and Caribbean English. But does that mean he simply switches from one to another according to the situation? As our questionnaire showed it is not as simple as that: many black pupils not only switch from one dialect to another but can also vary the intensity with which features of one or another appear in their speech.

3   INTER-SCHOOL DIVERSITY

Starting with the individual, we have built up a picture from a sample of twenty-eight London schools. Allowing for our *caveats* about the sample population (see pp. 45–50) this gave a hardness of definition to a picture which was hitherto blurred and distorted. The diversity has emerged from the shadows. That was a way of looking at the sample school population as a whole. There is, however, another way of looking at our sample which carries with it some significant implications. We can look at the differences between schools. Here, too, there were easily predicted differences. Any knowledgeable Londoner is aware of the concentrations of ethnic minorities in certain areas. He would have to be oblivious to disturbing events and the evidence of his eyes not to have assembled a rough-and-ready map. It follows, therefore, that schools will differ from each other in their diversity profiles as dramatically as individuals. Here, too, this predictable outcome is more impressive when we shift from general awareness to the detailed texture of the findings. Let us illustrate this by selecting four schools. We set out the facts in Figs. 1—4. The social setting of the schools (labelled A, B, C, D) may be briefly described as follows.

School A: An inner-London school in a working-class area which has experienced great population changes and has a large population of West Indian origin.

School B: An inner-London school in a working-class area which has remained virtually untouched by the demographic changes of inner-London. The population is, and has been for generations, very stable and constitutes a closely-knit community.

School C: An inner-London school of considerable social and ethnic variety. The area is typical of some inner-London settings in as much as a well-to-do and somewhat cosmopolitan population rubs shoulders with a working-class population, both white and black.

School D: An outer-London school in a borough which borders on suburbia in the north and is typically inner-London in the south. Thus the population contains a considerable social mix and some ethnic groups for whom the borough is an area of relatively concentrated settlement. For both schools C and D it would be a mistake to work with the formula that the category 'recently immigrant' is synonymous with the low-paid working class. We can compare these selected shcools, bearing in mind the thumb-nail descriptions, from several points of view.

In school A, the full London speakers are either black or white, in school B entirely white. Whereas many of the former will have something of a Caribbean dialect in their repertoires, a mere handful of the latter has any additional language resource.

The great variation in numbers of Standard speakers is another sharp reminder of school-to-school differences. The significant presence of Standard speakers in the peer group may make for important differences in how the target language is perceived by those for whom English is a second language.

What do these very impressive differences suggest in respect of policy? We shall go on to suggest several ways in which important decisions can be made at levels above the school, both locally and nationally and we do not wish to minimize

Figure 1: Principal language groups, based on first language or dialect in four schools

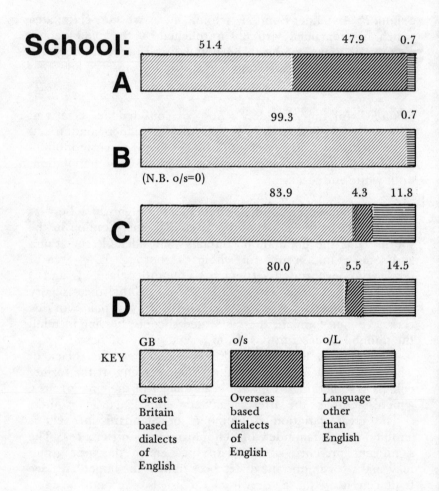

School:

A — 51.4 | 47.9 | 0.7

B — 99.3 | 0.7 (N.B. o/s=0)

C — 83.9 | 4.3 | 11.8

D — 80.0 | 5.5 | 14.5

KEY

GB — Great Britain based dialects of English

o/s — Overseas based dialects of English

o/L — Language other than English

Figure 2: Principal sub-groups of Great Britain-based dialects in four schools

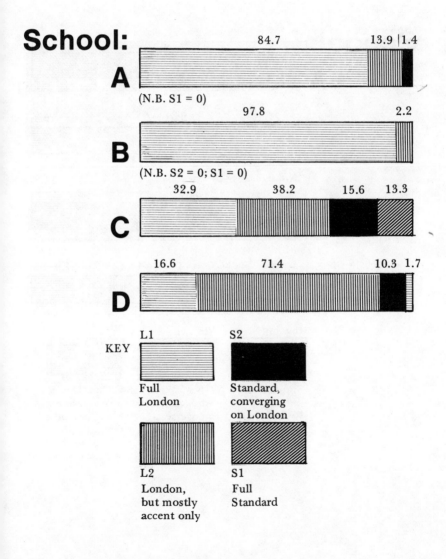

School:

A — 84.7 | 13.9 | 1.4
(N.B. S1 = 0)

B — 97.8 | 2.2
(N.B. S2 = 0; S1 = 0)

C — 32.9 | 38.2 | 15.6 | 13.3

D — 16.6 | 71.4 | 10.3 | 1.7

KEY

L1 — Full London

S2 — Standard, converging on London

L2 — London, but mostly accent only

S1 — Full Standard

101

Figure 3: Further dialects and languages spoken by GB speakers in four schools

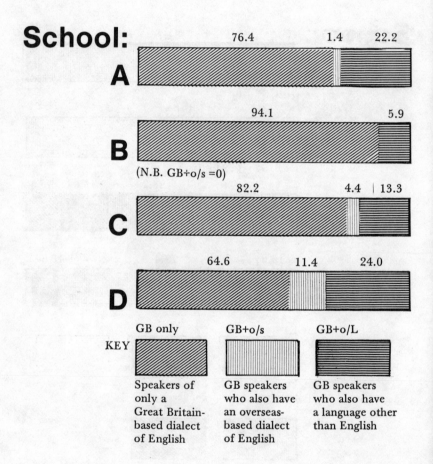

School:

A 76.4   1.4   22.2

B 94.1   5.9
(N.B. GB+o/s =0)

C 82.2   4.4 | 13.3

D 64.6   11.4   24.0

KEY

GB only — Speakers of only a Great Britain-based dialect of English

GB+o/s — GB speakers who also have an overseas-based dialect of English

GB+o/L — GB speakers who also have a language other than English

Figure 4: Principal Language Groups, when second languages and dialects are taken into account in **four** schools

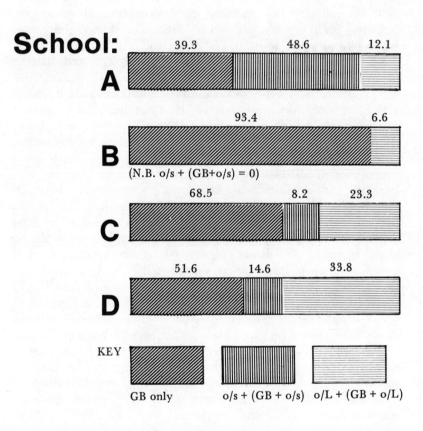

School:

A — 39.3 | 48.6 | 12.1

B — 93.4 | 6.6
(N.B. o/s + (GB+o/s) = 0)

C — 68.5 | 8.2 | 23.3

D — 51.6 | 14.6 | 33.8

KEY

GB only | o/s + (GB + o/s) | o/L + (GB + o/L)

the positive effects of those decisions. Nevertheless, at this point, we wish to emphasize that whatever is done to help, support and guide schools from outside, *nothing can relieve schools from the task of evolving a tailor-made policy and practice from the particular mix which confronts them.* We are sceptical about the results of authority *fiats* which attempt to lay down obligations, e.g. that any school which contains a group of pupils which speaks a language other than English and exceeding X in number must provide mother tongue teaching for Y hours per week within the school timetable. Each school must look to its own teaching resources, must come to an understanding of what both languages and dialects mean to the pupils and parents, must assess realistically what can be done, must define what kinds of additional help it needs. This approach matches precisely what has been found in the attempts to establish a 'language policy across the curriculum'. Clumsy efforts to push schools and teachers into policy-making before they had understood the underlying ideas and in conformity with official instruction have achieved nothing but hostility and bewilderment. Developing school practice which incorporates linguistic diversity is, after all, language across the curriculum realized in special circumstances. If it is a general principle that small group discussion is a vital aid to learning, what special steps need to be taken when the small group is far from homogeneous linguistically and culturally? If the language of science or mathematics creates special problems for the learner, are they the same for all linguistic groups in the school? *School-made language policy across the curriculum needs to be based on the particular diversity to be found in any one school.* If our conclusion is the right one, then that is fortunate. It happens that the facts of language in London schools require in the first place active involvement on the part of teachers rather than solutions which come from above or simple expedients like the appointment of a specialist. And the conditions are ripe for just such an approach. We found in almost every school a nucleus of teachers enthusiastic at the prospect of equipping themselves to adapt and enrich curricula to meet their particular form of diversity. The survey was itself a spur to this kind of initiative. It was also true, of course, that some schools had gone further in their thinking than others. There were some teachers with a deep understanding of some of the languages and dialects in their school and some schools

104

which had some sort of programme under way. For other schools, many of the issues raised by the survey were quite new. The progress from one way of thinking to the other cannot be telescoped.

To avoid misinterpretation we should add this. We have said nothing which implies that every school is a unique case, that schools do not share certain characteristics, that no outside intervention is to be welcomed, that teachers from different schools should not share experience and ideas. We enlarge these possibilities as we explore implications further. We have only wished to assert early in this chapter that no two schools are alike in respect of the precise configuration of linguistic diversity within them, that they are at different stages of awareness and understanding, that in the end each school will need its own detailed strategy and tactics built from its own experience. We have had some strong traditions which should make this procedure easier. We suggest that the agenda for school discussions will need to include:

   (i)   the means by which the languages and dialects of the pupils can be brought within the life of the school
  (ii)   specific forms of help to particular groups
 (iii)   literacy and reading
 (iv)   relationships between language and culture (the culture of the home and the culture of the school)
  (v)   language diversity across the curriculum
 (vi)   examinations, assessment and testing

Since the investigators and their investigation have had a secondary school bias we must add:

 (vii)   the importance of the mother tongue in the first years of schooling.

4   LANGUAGE MAINTENANCE

We discussed at the opening of this chapter the gap between declarations of intent and implementation in school practice. There is no escaping the fact that the languages and dialects of school pupils and how the educational system reacts to them is a political matter. Nowhere can this be seen more clearly than in Quebec. In several countries, the USA for example, it has become a question of federal law.

In February 1976 the EEC issued its Directive on the *Education of Migrant Workers' Children* which included provision for:

> organising and developing a reception system which would include intensive study of the language or languages of the host country

and

> Providing more opportunities as appropriate for teaching these children their mother tongue and culture, if possible in school and in collaboration with the country of origin.

These provisions, it should be noted, were to apply to 'the children of nationals of other Member States and of non-member countries'. There was considerable resistance to the scheme on the part of the British government which argued that in our system such decisions were a matter for local authorities rather than central government, that the emphasis on the 'children of migrant workers' was too narrow to meet the circumstances of ethnic minorities in Britain and that, such was the diversity of languages, it would be impossible to comply with a legal directive. There was also resistance from the National Union of Teachers on financial and professional grounds. But there were other aspects of the EEC directive which gave grounds for dissatisfaction. The wording made clear that language teaching was being linked to possible repatriation, i.e. that the strongest argument for mother tongue teaching was that it would ease the return of children to their countries of origin. In any case the directive is so generally phrased that it cannot indicate how it could be applied in the complex local circumstance nor does it clarify the educational, as distinct from political goals of the enterprise.

In 1977 the directive underwent significant revision. It removed the element of compulsion and the absolute legal right to mother tongue teaching and was accepted by the British government. What is desperately needed now is a clarification of the principles underlying our commitment and the development of realistic plans to fulfil it. It is one thing to give generous-minded assent to the educational principle that all children have the right to be taught their mother tongue and culture and quite another to decide by what methods and by means of what organization it should be carried out.

The arguments in favour of mother tongue teaching have, in our opinion, had a general force since we believe in multi-cultural education. On the other hand, if it means children being taught by unprepared teachers, possibly against their will, by mediaeval methods, it could do more harm than good. It would also be irresponsible to shut our eyes to other difficulties. Let us take one thorny problem. It is by no means clear what is meant by the 'mother tongue' of the pupils. We understand, for example, that the Punjabi spoken in this country has changed significantly and that this changed Punjabi is already finding its way into the printed form. This is the Punjabi children know. Is it the Punjabi they should be taught? Tosi (1979) has shown the peculiar difficulties of teaching Italian to children whose Italian is neither Standard nor the dialect of the region of origin. We are not competent to make pronouncements about such matters. We can, however, say that *policies should be based on careful linguistic and sociolinguistic studies of the languages as they function in this country.* We must remember too that the potential clientele does not consist simply of children for whom the non-English language is a second language but even possibly those who know very little of it, or perhaps nothing. We have also to reiterate that we cannot assume either a desire on the part of parents and children or agreement between parent and child. It must be clear that neither the model of foreign language teaching nor the model of mother tongue teaching meets the case. Undoubtedly the greatest difficulty is our collective ignorance of bilingualism. We shall therefore return to this theme, which was introduced in Chapter 2. Before doing so, however, there is a broader canvas against which language maintenance must be considered.

We are disposed to take a much broader view of language maintenance than is normally the case. Perhaps fostering would be a better term. We do so because our central concern is with the multi-cultural classroom. It is customary to think of language maintenance as meaning:

(i) teaching the language of a linguistic minority to those pupils who already speak it either within the national school system or by some other means

(ii) extending (i) to include the culture of the minority,

(iii) the use of the minority language as the medium of school learning and teaching all or some of the school curriculum for all or some of the pupil's school life.

No serious person would advocate the total substitution of another language for English within our school system. It follows therefore that language maintenance leaves us with the problems of how best to teach English as a second language, about which there is certainly no unanimity of view. Our wider view of language maintenance would extend to cover these possibilities:

(i) the provision of any facilities which enable groups or individuals to use their knowledge of a non-English language (conversation groups, films, tapes, books etc.)

(ii) the supportive process of fostering respect and interest in other languages, e.g. by the use of literature in translation

(iii) the confirmation of the pupils' culture and language throughout the curriculum and through the schools' facilities, especially their libraries and resource centres.

In other words, the choice is not simply between the provision of mother tongue classes and nothing. Any school would examine its practice and consider what is desirable and what is feasible.

Since we are attempting to take the broadest view of this question we should at this point ask whether it makes sense to separate language from dialects, especially overseas dialects, of English. If we are disposed to show respect for language which seems to us indisputably foreign, why should dialects be excluded from the same kind of consideration? There are reasons why an exact analogy cannot be made. Dialect culture is almost entirely an oral culture and its status in the eyes of its users is rarely high. However, there are important school activities such as drama, and the writing of stories and poems and the study of language in which the acceptance of dialect might be seen as language maintenance. We can already point to writing and improvised drama in London schools which would be both impoverished and pointless if it were purged of dialect, moreover, it would never have come into being without it.

What should be our policy for bilingual education? We have already suggested that no single formula like the EEC directive will cover the many different situations in our schools and that no direct line can be drawn from our figures to policy. At the same time it can be said that first and foremost a place should be found within our system for minority languages and appropriate resources allocated. Many of the speakers of minority languages are amongst the poorest inhabitants of the capital and bilingual education cannot work social miracles. It is only likely to make a lasting contribution if it occurs within a programme of multi-cultural education for all pupils. There may be some gains from little ghettos of pupils working away at Greek or Punjabi but they are likely to be very small. On the other hand at school reception age the failure to use a child's mother tongue can do lasting damage. If ghetto seems too strong a word, it should at least be recognized that one of the hazards of multi-cultural education is segregation in the cause of according rights to minorities. In our school system segregation is firmly installed. We segregate by sex, by age, by religion, by class, by attainment. We are not convinced that minority rights are best accommodated by adding to that pattern of segregation. The Coordinating Committee for Mother Tongue Teaching which is carrying out such valuable pioneer work will have to address itself to this issue.

In spite of all the complexities and difficulties we have outlined we suggest that there are steps which can reasonably be taken immediately:

(i) local authorities should know which of their schools contain minorities in sufficient numbers to justify the consideration of mother tongue classes within the curriculum.

(ii) local authorities should also compile list of teachers who could teach minority languages or be trained to do so

(iii) schools should take the initiative in starting classes and ask for the financial and other resources to sustain them

(iv) at all levels there is a need to pool resources. There are too many lonely improvisers. The experience of other countries should be made available to teachers (see Claydon *et al*, 1977)

We think that efforts of the kind we have outlined are most

likely to have beneficial effects if they are carried out in conjunction with others. Wright (1978) assessing the experience of the ILEA Bilingual Education Project sets these out with uncompromising directness:

    (i) the minority language must be of real use to the pupil within the school (e.g. as a medium of useful information)

   (ii) work done with the minority language should be integrated with the mainstream of classroom activity

  (iii) uses of translation and interpretation to give bilinguals a chance to use their resources as a contribution to the multi-cultural classroom

  (iv) the option of learning minority languages should be available for all pupils

   (v) the pupils themselves must choose whether or not to participate in courses.

5   IN-SERVICE TEACHER EDUCATION

As we proceeded with our research, we were more and more obliged to undertake our own education in linguistic diversity. We shared this need with most of those in what is usually thought of as 'the Teaching of English' (as distinct from foreign language teaching, the teaching of English as a foreign language or as a second language). Everything we have undertaken since we began our enquiry has underlined the need firstly to convince many more teachers of the central importance of the facts and what lies behind them and secondly to provide much more assistance in situations which place intolerable demands upon them. Almost none will have had as part of their training as teachers either a general linguistic education or one specifically directed towards a multi-cultural society. It is unreasonable to expect, therefore, a do-it-yourself understanding of the phenomena they encounter in their everyday teaching.

We are talking about teachers in inner-city schools who have to contend with some of the most testing circumstances in our school system. It would be only common justice to provide them with every possible support. *The clearest conclusion which emerges from our work is the need for in-service provision.* In-service courses take many different forms and are carried out by many different agencies. It is therefore not possible to describe one course which would meet all circumstances. We would suggest, however, that any substantial course would need to include the following themes:

(i) Language differences and within-language differences
(ii) Bilingualism
(iii) Bidialectalism
(iv) Interlanguage
(v) Attitudes to language and language loyalty
(vi) Literacy for second-language learners and second-dialect learners (especially Standard written English)
(vii) The study of language in the school curriculum
(viii) Language and multi-cultural education.

In-service education of this kind should have an organic and direct link with the schools from which the teachers are drawn and with the pupils with whom they work. *There is a strong case to be made out for a carefully planned and monitored pilot or model course* based on a small group of schools. It should be the aim of such courses not only to equip teachers with increased understanding, but also to aim at the formulation of policy, detailed plans of work and programmes for the participant schools.

6   EXAMINATION AND TESTS

The examination system in secondary schools is in the melting pot. The Assessment of Performance Unit is embarking on the first testing programme of its kind launched by the central government in Britain. Some teachers are deeply concerned with what the next few years will produce, yet there is little evidence that any major changes and innovations looming on the horizon have sufficiently taken into consideration the needs of many groups of pupils who exist in such large numbers in the schools. Examination systems are, perhaps inevitably, very conservative and therefore not swiftly responsive to changes in the schools. It is a justifiable assumption that taken as a whole, examinations say to the schools, 'It is the children who must change, not us'. In other words, the traditional assimilationist attitudes we have noted in other contexts leave their mark here too. Teachers who have worked in multi-cultural schools are naturally the first to insist that for children who are bilingual or speakers of dialect, examinations are a central issue. Reform the curriculum how you may, if examinations in effect operate in a discriminatory fashion and consequently fail to do justice to particular categories of children, the best of efforts in schools will seem like a fraud or palliative. How could it be anything else when such an emphasis is placed on examinations?

We find ourselves here in a common predicament, the predicament of so many teachers. The examination system can scarcely be considered as uniformly benign, particularly in its influence on the curriculum. Nevertheless, since the life-chances of pupils hang upon it, teachers have to come to terms with it and attempt to change it in ways which do more justice to their pupils' talents and resources. Our view of the examination system in the context of this report may seem like a relatively narrow one. Yet it is one important exemplar of the ways in which examinations and tests impose constraints in some way or another upon all pupils. Those who may differ vehemently from us in this view should nevertheless not be blind to the particular hardships which the system imposes on some pupils, nor to the protracted neglect of their interests and they should be able to join us in considering some necessary changes. We, for our part, must acknowledge that the system has been sufficiently flexible to embrace the concept of 'Mode 3' by means of which schools can develop their own programmes of work to meet the needs and interests of their own pupils. This means that there are precedents for accommodating the needs of pupils even though few initiatives have yet been made.

It is notoriously difficult to assess language use. Course work and oral work have allowed, at least, for a broader view of language functions and language competence, just as Mode 3s have encouraged a more generous view of literature for school. The stubborn obstacles still remain. The classic pattern of examinations, in English and other subjects, rests heavily on mastery of Standard written English and perhaps even a narrow view of that. There are children who make a striking success of a transition from a dialect or another language to the literary or technical English required in higher education. They may have special good fortune during the transition. There is some evidence that amongst children who are in the third phase of learning English (which we can loosely define as moving from fluency-with-foreignness to speaking-like-a-native) those who speak a standard version of their mother tongue and are literate in it are likely to do better in our examinations than those who speak a dialect and are not literate, even though both groups may be equally competent in English. The pupils in our survey would overwhelmingly come into the second category. The path has not been smoothed for them through the good fortune of life circumstances which in some senses are compatible with our examination system.

We have said that the proposals which are current for changing our national system of examinations have not conspicuously registered the existence of the second language and second dialect learners. Yet it would be obvious justice to ask that their interests should be reckoned with and their attainments be given due recognition. Can we persuade the examination system to register that a pupil who has understood an important principle and expresses it comprehensibly, but foreignly, is in fact displaying a double achievement — learning the principle of expressing it in a second language? We are certainly not asking for easy options, bonuses for the handicapped or late-starters. Actually that idea is not outrageous, but raises more practical and political difficulties than we can deal with. We must also reckon with the fact that many of the pupils and their parents will want to participate straightforwardly in British society on its own terms and would be angry to be treated as in need of benevolent special pleading. What we are proposing is that certification should be genuinely informative and we must search out ways of registering achievements and abilities which have been ignored. If the curriculum needs to be broadened, then the examination system, by the same token, does too. Knowledge of Ibo, of Islamic thought, of Indian literature, of Caribbean folk stories, music and dance, for instance, are assets in national as well as individual terms. So too, it hardly needs saying, is a flexible and confident use of the English language. One need not preclude the other.

The diversity of cultures and languages in contemporary Britain points in the direction of a broader and more flexible curriculum. Changes in curriculum point in their turn to an examination system which is sensitive to those changes, which recognizes hitherto unrecognized talents, and which scrutinizes its practices for ethnocentricity and remoteness.

At whatever age a child first starts to learn English as a second language he or she will be moving from a first one. That child cannot simply mark time in a language-less vacuum while English is learned. For many children who are born here or who have taken on English at an early age, the mother tongue may wither in importance, either as a consequence of parental insistence or because the language of peers, school and the community is so emphatically English that the mother tongue may come to seem no more than a relic of childhood, redolent of a primitive or possibly ineffectual way of life. Many adults who are bilingual testify to having in their teens regarded their mother tongue in this light, as some vestigial repository of childhood and a folklore culture, although they were often anxious to relearn and use that language when they were only a little older. Teachers involved in mother tongue teaching, retention or maintenance have testified to the ambiguities involved in defining the term mother tongue and to the kinds of resistance children may show to outside encouragement to use their home language. Nonetheless, there are many children for whom the mother tongue or home dialect continues to exercise a profound effect on their learning, and it is an effect which can be allowed to be unhelpful.

To start with, let us take the example of a child arriving in the fourth or fifth year of secondary school, having interrupted an education differing noticeably from what is on offer here. That child, and that child's family may be experiencing all the practical and emotional difficulties of being uprooted and then planted in a new and alien culture. The child will be expected to learn English, with a curriculum directed towards fifth-year examinations. He will need more time, and possibly financial help, in order to fulfil his potential within the English school system. There are some subjects which he might be able to study, and be examined in, in his own language, either by continuing courses which he had already begun at home or by following adapted versions of courses taught here.

It is possible to take many of the languages spoken by minority groups here at O level. Most of these examinations are modelled on the foreign language papers taken in French, say, by native English pupils. These have two disadvantages. They require, in general, a ludicrously low level of knowledge of the language concerned (ludicrous, that is, for speakers of the language) but depend on a fairly sophisticated knowledge of English. Children's experience of their home country, culture and language is unlikely to be adequately mirrored in exercises requiring translations, some exercises in structure and two or three hundred words of continuous prose. It is absurd to suppose that a child who speaks and understands Cantonese and can read and write it only deserves a certificate to say he can do these things if he can also prove that he can translate what he knows into English. The principle here needs constant reiteration. That child can do things and knows things which are invaluable to him and to our society. They should be validated. He is also going to need to operate the English language and to participate confidently in the culture of the country he is living in. Not only does the first not preclude the second, but the second depends vitally upon the first. Some children may never have learned their parents' mother tongue, others may forget it and wish to relearn it. For them, examinations in these languages on the model of our foreign languages examinations may be suitable. A society like ours needs teachers who speak more than one language. One way of ensuring that we get such teachers is to capitalize on the language resources the country already possesses by validating at several levels languages with which children are acquainted when they come to school.

The same principle can be applied to the evaluation of knowledge and skills in other parts of the curriculum. There are schools which have introduced Asian studies into their CEE work, and others which have negotiated 'Mode 3s' with particular examination boards to allow for a study of Caribbean literature. It is possible to imagine a syllabus for history, geography, social studies, religious knowledge and domestic science examinations from CSE to A level standard which would include sizeable options on, for example, Turkish history, industrialization of parts of the Third World, Islamic studies or a comparison of domestic customs in different parts of the world. This is not a prescription for cultivating nothing but your own back garden or for small-scale chauvinism, but a suggestion for building a programme of diversity and relativism into the curriculum provided for all children. And the other side of the coin would be a determined effort to eradicate cultural bias which is bound to be disabling for many children and an ethnocentricity, or Eurocentricity, which is disabling for us all. From an educational point of view these would be moves which would have at least three major advantages: they would build concretely on the diverse experiences which our pupils bring to their schooling; they would enrich the curriculum for all children; and they would provide a more realistic preparation for living and working in a multi-cultural Britain.

The question of how best to assess the progress or achievement of a pupil who is learning English as a second language is a different but no less crucial one. It has already been suggested that it should partly be dealt with in the context of language teaching and assessment generally. That is, it involves, as language assessment for all children does, a recognition of a range of language activities which should be valued in the curriculum. There is a hazard implicit here, which is that, if a skill or an activity can only be validated for schools by its incorporation into an examination system, there might come to be almost no language activity indulged in which did not find its counterpart in the assessment process. It has been argued that the introduction of oral examining has had the beneficial effect of encouraging schools to look at more than written language, and to value a variety of spoken modes, as well as listening and response. The danger is that assessment may intervene to prevent genuine language going on. In ordinary life, after all, there is no more disconcerting response to something we may say than an assessment of how we said it. Nonetheless, a much broader view of what the language skills of children are and even of what they ought to be is beginning to prevail. Many an examination syllabus differentiates in a more positive way between written and spoken language functions. The bland assumption that we can test oral or reading comprehension by setting a few questions is weakening. Dialect, for many teachers, is no longer a bastard form to be expunged and replaced. More thought is given to the relation between spoken and written forms and between both those forms and other processes of mind. It could not be said that most English language papers adequately reflect this new awareness. Most of them adhere a good deal more closely to presumed norms of what employers want and need and what is required by a higher education based on literacy.

There are by now several syllabuses (and proposals for more) for examining English as a second language. These have different emphases. Most are modelled to some extent on a view of the way second languages are most often taught; as a series of structures to be learnt in isolation, usually as unrelated to

116

another language or languages, which can be simply ordered from easier to more difficult items, and so on. Some see a kind of hierarchy of language functions, which begin with something in the nature of 'survival language' and move upwards to something else called 'the language of education'. With some exceptions, the stress is on written forms and on accuracy, rather than on spoken language to use and make sense of. Most of the syllabuses regard the language pupils need and use to think, recall, imagine and speculate as secondary to the language needed to write, say, a letter of application or pass an examination. Only one syllabus we know of proposes that the learning of English as a second language goes on within a bilingual context. None, as far as we know, sees the learning of first and second languages within the context of multi-culturalism, so that literature, film, television, sport and school activities of all kinds both contribute to and motivate language learning. 'Usefulness' is not to be sneered at, but it is a difficult idea to wield with conviction, and the drawback of most of the proposals for assessing attainment in English as a second language is that the acquisition of such a 'useful' language is divorced from the sorts of processes in first language learning which allow us to become the best judges finally of what is 'useful' to us for particular purposes. There seems to be, however, a need for certification to mark the stages of second language learning.

At its starkest, this need, attested by teachers in sixth forms and Further Education Colleges, is for an O level certificate (or its equivalent) for students pursuing studies in other subjects, who need such a qualification for a job or further training. Both CEE and CSE provide scope for manoeuvre in terms of the kinds of literature and culture which might be studied and for a variety of written and spoken tasks. Neither they nor O level, however, sets out to elicit from candidates more than a restricted sample of language use, and that sample tends to be representative of the kind of language most remote from the language of conversation or of thought. So there are students who might, for instance, have good grades at A level in maths or science subjects, who are still incapacitated by a failure to pass an English examination. The other area of need may be a more transitional one, where certification is needed to guarantee for employers a high level of progress in English learning which provides grounds for expecting that a young person is likely to become proficient in time, given the right experience and encouragement. Again, this proposes a level of attainment and of validation which is realistic in terms of the student's engagement with the language at that moment. CSE, with its stress on a large collection of writing, personal and formal, can present such a learner with insuperable problems. This is not because imaginative language is beyond him, but because he is learning language in action and in order to do things in his life. One of the most imaginative draft proposals for a syllabus for this group of young people concentrates on the collection on tapes of examples of language in a variety of situations; examples which they might use as models as well as for study in terms of function and register. Many of the pupils we are discussing, who might in one way or another be described as either bilingual or bidialectal, have skills which vastly transcend ·those of their teachers or their monolingual classmates. They may be able to shift, to adopt a metalinguistic approach to the differences and similarities between languages and dialects, to develop a whole extra range of interpretative and performing skills, which are in no way rewarded by the examinations as they stand. What is needed, then, is not a range of easier options for such students, but a flexible scheme for assessing a far wider range of skills and knowledge than is currently thought worthy of being honoured by certification.

Impatience with the present system of examining school students is shared by people who have vastly different reasons for wanting things changed. It would, nevertheless, be a tragedy if these changes were allowed to happen without reference to what is probably the most important complex of events to affect this country in the twentieth century. We need a different examination system because we are a different kind of society, and we need one as well because we have endured for far too long a system which relies on techniques for detecting inadequacy and insists on failure. There are things we need to find out. Any serious investigation into what is actually involved in acquiring the language competence which is considered acceptable to employers and educators must be accompanied by just as serious an investigation into the array of language abilities which children in fact possess. There exists a growth industry in examinations, of a usually vocational orientation, which offers certification for English as a foreign language and English as a second language. Such proliferation needs to be scrutinized in the context of language learning and assessment generally and in relation to the central role language plays in social, cultural and educational experience. To pay attention to the advantages and the disadvantages enjoyed by children who are bidialectal or bilingual is to do no more than accept that the examination industry, like many other aspects of education in this country, has inclined towards a too simple and monolithic an account of social priorities and of their solution. Should the present proposal for a single examination at 16+ and the introduction of N and F levels become realities, these new examinations must be judged by the extent to which they take account of the matters we have been discussing.

7 LANGUAGE DIVERSITY AS PART OF THE LANGUAGE CURRICULUM

During our work we derived great satisfaction from the interest taken by many pupils in our enquiry. While it was our deliberate intention that they should see it in a positive light, we had not anticipated that we would be questioned so frequently about languages and dialects. Assumptions were made about our linguistic omniscience which were flattering but unjustified. A completely unforeseen by-product of our work grew out of this interest. We had made the suggestion that one way of collecting the information we needed would be to introduce some basic ideas of diversity to the selected classes and that they could then assemble the data relating to themselves. One school took up this idea with enthusiasm and it was suggested that linguistic diversity was, if handled imaginatively, a potentially rich curriculum resource, and that language diversity of all kinds could be the core of language study. Teachers were quick to point out that any sustained effort of this kind could not be improvised. It was both uneconomic and difficult for small groups of teachers to assemble materials and to shape a new curriculum. Accordingly, a working party was set up. A very short time after its inception we were able, in June 1978, to organize a conference based on documents and materials assembled by them. The working party is still actively functioning and this section of our report is very much theirs. *This work on curriculum materials for the study of linguistic diversity and the development of a rationale is a most promising development. With financial support it could make a major contribution to the reform of language study in schools and at the same time*

119

to multi-cultural education.

This is no place to discuss the scope of language study in the curriculum. We shall have to content ourselves by noting the vacuum left by the widespread abandonment of traditional grammar teaching. In general, the emphasis of English teaching has been on developing a capacity to use language well by using it rather than learning about language and its structure. Much of the criticism of the study of language in school has been based on its inadequate view of what language is and how it works, on the premature introduction of abstract concepts, its lack of effect on language performance. Bearing this in mind, we can take a closer look at some new possibilities.

The working party set out to show how their pupils' languages and dialects, those too often left at the school gates, were not problems, but a rich, natural resource for learning about language and languages. Language diversity can mean something multi-dimensional. It can mean, for instance, varieties of English: dialects, group languages, slangs and jargons and styles, private language, anti-languages, non-verbal languages, as well as the languages associated with sex and age and class and occupation. And it can mean, most especially, languages which are not English. In this way, diversity would include all the uses of language, in which all children, for most of the time, are skilled practitioners. Partly, this would be a matter of making public and explicit what teachers are beginning to understand. If some areas of linguistic study have been helpful to teachers, then it is time, perhaps, for pupils — some of whom have broader language experiences than many of their teachers — to be let in on the act. It is a double act, really, which uses diversity as productive and important in itself, while encouraging a view of language as a system which, more than any other, unites human beings; something they most extraordinarily have in common.

This programme for language teaching would centre on activities designed to explore language in action, language as it is used, though there would be scope for reflection on the nature of language, of its written forms, its relation to thought, its first appearance in young children. Such a programme would generate its own material and subject matter, so that general features of language could be studied as it is used, in all its variety, in the shifts and combinations of styles and registers which characterize language in its communal uses, as well as in its place within individual development.

Central to such a programme are attitudes to language: ideas about correctness, appropriateness, effectiveness. Children who are to develop as successful, confident users of language have to be encouraged to look beyond habits and prejudices, too often endorsed without explanation by teachers, examinations and employers, to the nature and implications of judgments about 'good' and 'bad' language. Children need to be aware of the ways in which language can exert power or confirm weakness. By exploring the functions and effects, as well as the constraints, of forms of spoken and written language, children may be enabled to revalue their own skills, gain much needed confidence through an appreciation of their ability to make sense of language in different modes, to move between dialects, styles, accents themselves and to interpret intention and motive from the language they attend to in others. These skills, and others, for mimicry, expressiveness and organization, for instance, are ones possessed by most children already, though a constricted view of language study can disguise them. There were many teachers who felt that by concentrating on them they themselves were more likely to discover how to help the pupils do those things they could not do yet.

It can be made to sound too easy. Language may be the pivot of human culture, it is also the touchstone of divisiveness, an area which is fraught with possibilities for pain and embarrassment. In the early days of developing the materials it was found that asking a couple of Chinese children to present a version of a story in their own language to a multi-ethnic classroom met with stubborn and articulate refusal. English children, they believed, would laugh at the story's supernatural happenings, too many things needed explaining. That episode exemplified for many teachers the problems as well as the scope of the undertaking. It made it clear, above all, that before any of the work they were proposing could go on they would have to make their classrooms places where such contributions were known to be welcome. The connections between languages and the connections between stories from different places and times have to be established, not theoretically but practically. There may be common reasons for telling stories and for the presence in them of common themes and forms and values, but the people who tell them do so in the belief that they and their hearers or readers have particular purposes and particular experiences to share. 'Language diversity' must not be a Babel, but grounds for making sense and order out of what has been allowed to remain a damaging confusion for thousands of children. It is a confusion which, at one level, allows 'O level language' or a letter of application, say, to embody 'good' English, while the speech which children first acquired, first confronted the world with, and which they now use with their families and with their friends, is accounted 'bad'. It is not a matter of introducing people who have come to live in this country to 'our' cultural heritage (a complex, controversial and, at times, hazy concept), since their arrival has, in any case, altered that 'our' irrevocably. The purpose is to take an entirely fresh look at what we share and at what we need to share from now on if we are to extend the capacities of all children to understand the nature of culture and of language, and to be free of the constraints inherent in both those forces while learning how to use them for their own purposes.

Before describing in detail the materials which have been produced and used in some multi-ethnic classrooms in London schools, it is worth mentioning one other matter. There were some teachers in the group who felt initially that such work might be difficult or even irrelevant in classrooms with a relatively monolingual population. Their doubts turned out to be unnecessary. Work which took diversity as its starting point could not fail to find such diversity. The materials have been used in schools and in classes where more than half the pupils were bilingual and where, therefore, as many as a dozen languages were spoken; and in classrooms where all the children spoke English as a mother tongue, although they also possessed a variety of dialects of English, both overseas and homegrown ones.

The materials

All the teachers involved in the creating and the using of the materials started from the survey, with collecting evidence of diversity. This, in itself, generated questions and suggested distinctions and categories. What is a mother tongue, for instance? The prevalence of a range of bilingualism and bidialectalism made this a difficult question to answer, even as it elicited, a wealth of varied experiences. What do you think of the language or the dialect you speak and what do you think other people think of it? Or, which of your two languages or dialects do you think would be more appropriate in particular situations or with particular people? Answering questions like these has led inevitably to discussion of the status of particular languages and of the reasons people have for making judgments about them.

The next stage has often been to tape speech of different sorts produced by pupils and to listen, refine and modify such judgments. Groups of children have improvised plays on tape in different languages and dialects, translating for each other, registering the ways in which a dialect of English may produce differences of accent, structure, vocabulary, behaviour and even character. There were teachers who made use of the original survey or devised modified versions of it to get the pupils themselves, in pairs or small groups, to compile information about the languages they spoke without teacher intervention, and this effectively highlighted the queries which are bound to come up in the process of deciding how to describe any individual's linguistic biography. One English department prepared for the survey by running a series of assemblies on the theme of the children's multi-cultural background. They displayed a chart to show the various flags of the countries represented. Another school is preparing to produce a booklet about the languages spoken by its pupils and to include in it useful information about school and the community as well as stories written in the different languages. Display and discussion of the wealth of dialects and languages a school or class could boast, as well as the high incidence of bilingualism, and multilingualism produced considerable pride, even competitiveness, and allowed for a demonstration of some consummate imitative skills.

The group has collaborated to produce a booklet called *Languages*,* which uses the classroom's languages to look at the diversity of languages in the world as a whole. It proposes work on families of languages, on the history, changes and borrowings of English and other languages. There are sections on languages with written forms and ones with none, and on the implications of different alphabetic forms and on the other kinds of symbolic systems used to convey information and ideas. For some teachers this has led to a consideration of the effects of literacy on societies, to discussion of what the ability to learn and use language tells us about human beings and societies. Another section deals imaginatively with the

*The booklet is being used by the group and others as trial material. It is hoped that a published version will eventually appear.

virtues and the difficulties of insisting upon a standard spelling. This work uses dialect writing and encourages activities where children will work together to invent, improve or explore spelling systems.

The materials include tapes of children and adults telling stories in dialect and in other languages, and these have been used to discuss stories and storytelling, to explore questions about veracity, narrative authority, shaping, persuasion and implicit point of view. Using these tapes again, children have been asked to translate, interpret, paraphrase and transcribe. They have been asked to speculate about a speaker's age, biography and circumstances, to match faces and houses with examples of speech and to investigate their attitudes to speakers and to the features of a speaker's performance from which they derive these attitudes.

An outstanding benefit of the work has been its collaborative nature and the scope it allows for children to teach each other. Children have been encouraged to teach other people something about their own language, for example its written form, words for numbers or colours or days of the week. Some children have brought into school newspapers and magazines in their home languages and books they have outgrown. The *Language* booklet suggests work for whole classes as well as for individuals. A class might, for instance, make a collection of oral and written stories, and this would involve them in transcribing and translating. The formal properties of language can be looked at comparatively. What knowledge is required to produce questions or use negatives or tenses or plurals? Do other languages mark these features in the same way? The usefulness of punctuation can also be looked at through a comparison with the way other languages operate. A selection of ideas involving codes, nonsense verse, invented words, alphabets or even grammars, rhyming slang, onomatopoeic language, bowdlerisms or malapropisms are also presented in ways which would encourage a teacher to help children to discover the formal properties of language rather than lecturing them. Children are encouraged to examine jargons and kinds of rhetoric and to describe and evaluate their use by, say, sports commentators, fashion writers, politicians, teachers, disc-jockeys. This has produced some imaginative drama work; and in general drama has turned out to be an ideal way of exploring the conceptual underpinning of language, verbal as well as non-verbal, while developing confidence in using language in ways which allow us to interpret it.

This list of possible language activities inspired by this work, an account of the writing and the speech and the dialogue it has inspired, and a look at the insights produced by it in teachers and pupils could go on forever. In many ways this approach to language teaching thrives on itself. It is not costly and it produces its own resources. Nonetheless, resources are needed, and it would be churlish to pretend that where this work has gone on it has not made use of what can be expensive books and other materials. BBC language programmes for schools have been plundered, and Thames Television's *The English Programme* with its accompanying booklet, *Language*, has been an invaluable source of ideas. The work is necessarily dependent on talk, and this means using tape, video and film at least as much as it means books, pens and paper. All the teachers involved in the project have expressed a need for dictionaries, for books (textbooks and story books) written in the languages of their pupils. There is a need for adult speakers of these languages to teach, tell stories, interpret and translate. It is not difficult to see how a teacher-initiated and teacher-run innovation of this kind could become both more ambitious and more widely disseminated with adequate funding.

The Australian experience, recounted in *Curriculum and Culture*, (Claydon *et al*, 1977), has much to offer teachers in urban and multi-cultural schools here, on two counts. In their *School Education Materials Project* they have produced curriculum material based on two principles which seem fundamental for future developments. The first is that using the languages of their pupils and helping them either with English or with a flourishing or diminishing mother tongue might be much more effectively done through teaching about subjects other than language. So far their work has been confined roughly to a territory which might be described as social studies, and has concentrated on the children's experience of the demands made by the community in which they live. It is possible to see an extension of the kind of work they are engaged in into virtually every area of the curriculum. The second principle has been that of using bilingual material within the classroom. This involves the possibility for each child to learn through double texts or bilingual tapes to approach a subject area through English or through his mother tongue, or, as he becomes more confident, through a combination of both. This has seemed to the teachers involved in developing material for multi-cultural mixed-ability classes the necessary next step.

Finally, to charges that this way of welcoming and capitalizing on diversity is no more than 'tokenism', barely touching on the problems underlying vital aspects of language learning in our urban schools, these teachers would wish to reply that the work itself has been stimulating, productive and illuminating for teacher and learner. They would readily agree that when a Greek-speaking child teaches his class some Greek words, thereby introducing to them some skills such as translating, interpreting, comparison and transliteration, this is by no means the only way of addressing the needs of a child in need of special help with English or of another who requires encouragement to learn or maintain his mother tongue. The situation cries out for diversity of provision, not for single solutions. But the teachers who have been involved in this work would also want to insist that the using of linguistic diversity within the classroom has vitally important implications for education within a multi-cultural society. It allows for the modifying of attitudes to languages and to dialects in ways which could be central to combat racism and prejudice generally. It also proposes a study of language based on pupils' own knowledge and experience, and in so doing forges links between school and community which can only enhance the curriculum.

8   SUPPORT FOR TEACHERS

It has been a reiterated theme of this report that it is totally unreasonable to expect teachers, however committed, to make a positive response to linguistic diversity without a supportive structure. The first tier of that support is the school itself. This can be seen at first as a matter of staffing and the distribution of resources. But staffing and the distribution of resources rest on policy-making. We cannot see how fundamental changes can be brought about without the involvement of most teachers in a school in the formulation of new policy. All this has been said before, ever since the ideas of a language policy across the curriculum first came into circulation. There is, however, a difference. The need for new kinds of provision is made much more glaring by the presence of pupils for whom the English language is a barrier to learning. It may be that this is seen simply as 'their English is not good enough' but that is at least a starting point. It also reminds us how much the issues we have been looking at apply to all pupils in one form or another, or at least to all pupils who are not mother tongue speakers of Standard English. They too are pupils of whom it is so often said 'their English is not good enough'. To simplify starkly we could say that centrally we are concerned with the vernacular speech of working-class children and its significance in learning. London is the great settlement area for ethnic minorities and most of them work in the poorer paid jobs. Whereas we could quite simply have thought of London working-class speech as Cockney we obviously can no longer do so. What does this mean for schools in working-class areas? It has been said in the past that curriculum has failed to acknowledge the experience and values of working-class pupils. This now takes on a more complex and challenging meaning and proposes to schools an exacting programme of reshaping and revision. Teachers as isolated individuals cannot undertake that task, only collective policy-making can do it.

It is from such discussions that there emerges a desperate need for more information. No teacher shouldering the heavy responsibilities and harassing pressures of teaching in an inner-city school can pick his or her way through the intimidating linguistic literature even if it were accessible. *There is an urgent need for well-produced manuals, booklets, films, tapes, etc. specifically designed for a teacher audience.* A few linguists have in recent years taken an interest in education but there is very little indication amongst linguistic scholars of a desire to assist in necessary popularization. We can already sketch some of the possibilities:

(i) In Chapter 1 we gave some indications of what it is useful to know about languages and dialects. What we need to know depends on the motives of our enquiry. The teacher's motives may overlap with the linguist's, but they will not coincide. With collaboration, a set of manuals could be produced which would provide teachers with illuminating insights into the languages most commonly encountered in schools. Take Greek, for example. What differences are there between Cypriot

Greek and mainland Greek? What are the attitudes of Greek speakers to these differences? What are the differences between 'Dhimotiki' and 'Katharevousa'? What is known about the literate culture of Greek people in England (newspapers, books, religious works, etc.)? What works in English translation would be most useful to read? What are the special difficulties encountered by Greek learners of English?

(ii) It is perhaps even more important that short teacher-directed texts on aspects of West Indian dialects should be prepared. Whereas teachers may readily acknowledge Greek (with its classical overtones) as worthy of respectful attention, West Indian dialects of English strongly rooted in an oral tradition, will not command the same kind of attention. Moreover, there is, as yet, relatively little awareness amongst teachers of language diversity in the Caribbean which is undergoing sustained study. Finally, teachers would be helped by a careful description of the changes which come over Caribbean dialects in the British setting. Edwards (1979) is a first contribution.

(iii) Given the widespread use of video and audio tapes, there is a disappointing paucity of tapes which would serve the purposes of teachers. The tapes of Great Britain based dialects are in many ways unsatisfactory. Priority should be given to tapes which show stages and aspects of 'inter-language' in school ESL learners, variations in the individual dialect speaker including code switching, pupils and adults talking about their attitudes to language. We have made no attempt to be exhaustive but simply to give some substance to a firm recommendation. *A national body should be formed which would:*

(a) *assess the needs for teacher-directed materials on linguistic diversity*
(b) *facilitate the production of such materials*
(c) *arrange for dissemination*

We suspect that if such materials were produced their use would go far beyond the one we have specified.

We have drawn attention to the fact that it is very difficult in most schools for pupils who can read and write another language to make use of it in the context of school learning.

While it may be easy to censure some schools for their reluctance to purchase books for such pupils, any criticism should be tempered by the fact that they are confronted by an almost impossible task of locating sources, selection and evaluation. Let us suppose that a Turkish speaking pupil is also interested in biology. Where do you obtain Turkish biology books appropriate for the pupil's age and attainment? There is no shortage of bad books in any language and, in addition, some countries have no strong tradition of well-produced children's books. Multiply this task for the teacher and what can he do but *despair*? Should he be heroic and tireless, the process would still be intolerably wasteful. There have been several initiatives in the compilation of resources lists and there are in some local authorities centres which have helped teachers in their search for materials, but they do not meet the case as we have outlined it. Quite simply, teachers must be able to draw upon supplies quickly and easily. *We therefore suggest that at local authority level there should be supplies of carefully selected materials in the major languages of minorities in the area.* Some national coordination would be an obvious advantage. Teachers should be able to draw on this book bank as and when they need to do so. Schools with a clear pattern of repeated use, for example, a consistent group of readers of Arabic, could bring up their own stocks. We have been influenced in making this suggestion by the clear evidence from teacher informants that again and again children arrive in their classrooms with little or no English.

The need for books goes beyond supplying the classroom. It extends to the shelves of school and local libraries. Some of the same problems arise. What should go on those shelves?

So far we have stressed that direct help which the provision of books can offer but just as important is the symbolic significance for the pupil of a school library or classroom which accepts and uses his language.

9 DIALECT AND STANDARD ENGLISH

Any discussion of the speaking of non-Standard English in schools generates unruly passions. Putting aside prejudiced and often irrational onslaughts of the vernacular speech of the overwhelming majority of pupils (79 per cent in our sample) which stigmatize it as lazy, ungrammatical or ugly, the serious and sustained argument has been that to learn to speak Standard is a social and economic necessity in contemporary Britain. Standard, so the argument runs, confers on its speakers access to the most extensive social and geographical space. Whereas at one time this was thought to be a justification for supplanting dialect speech, the more tolerant view is now that Standard should be added to the pupil's repertoire. The Bullock Report (HMSO, 1975), as we might expect, advances this solution in its most persuasive and enlightened form:

> The aim is not to alienate the child from a form of language with which he has grown up and which serves him effectively in the speech community of his neighbourhood. It is to enlarge his repertoire so that he can use language effectively in other speech situations and use standard forms when they are needed. (p. 143)

Certainly this is just what many parents would like schools to undertake. If the goal is acceptable, is it also attainable? A recent work (Gregory and Carroll, 1978) sees no difficulties:

> ... we can suggest that it would be entirely possible for all members of a community to speak a standard variety regardless of their social standing.

However, we shall need to have explained to us how, while maintaining sound principles for the teaching of English, we can teach spoken Standard. Furthermore, it is difficult to imagine a deliberate pedagogy which would not produce many recognizably second-class speakers of Standard, Standard in a limbo where linguistic anxiety stifles spontaneous speech. For more that a century there has been no shortage of advocates for teaching spoken Standard in school. Incalculable pupil-teacher hours have been expended in the attempt to banish 'ain't', 'we was' and the so-called double negative, all to little or no purpose except perhaps to implant doubt and even shame where none existed before. It should go without saying that the capacity to *comprehend* Standard English is quite another matter since all children have sufficient contact through the media, their teachers and other sources to develop the necessary receptive competence. Throughout this report both implicitly and explicitly we have made it clear that we would give priority

130

to all measures which give pupils confidence in those codes which are both effective systems and bearers of significant and powerful meaning. If we can support, as many now do, hospitality towards diversity of languages then it is logical to extend it to diversity of dialects.

Easily said. Even if attitudes to dialect in the classroom were mellowing into tolerance and perhaps enthusiasm, we would still have to confront some issues which need exploration. Amongst the growing band of teachers who welcome the spontaneous use of vernacular speech, there are discussions and doubts which rapidly rise to the surface. In the main these concern (a) West Indian speech (b) reading (c) the writing of dialect and Standard.

West Indian speech
We have dealt at some length with the complexities of West Indian speech in its British setting and will not repeat our discussion here. In many respects the school's response should be no different from its response to all vernacular speech. Trudgill (1979) and Edwards (1979) have, however, drawn attention to the fact that those West Indian children whose language is close to Creole may experience special difficulties. Trudgill suggests: 'Even long-term exposure . . . may not be too effective in the case of profound grammatical differences'. He concludes:

> Even this evidence [i.e. from Edwards, 1976, that for some children 'Creole interference leads to comprehension difficulties'. Ed.], however, does not really argue for the teaching of Standard English in schools. The West Indians who have this type of difficulty have problems not simply with Standard English but with British English as a whole. And, except perhaps in the case of new arrivals who might be favourably disposed to such an exercise, there would clearly be resistance to attempts to withdraw some West Indians from classes for special attention. Much more helpful would be a recognition, especially by teachers, that some West Indian children in British schools may be faced with what is best described as a semi-foreign language problem. (It is probably also true to say that the main problem is the belief, widely held by West Indians and British people alike, that native West Indian dialects are

'bad' or 'broken'.)

As we have shown the group to which these comments apply is a small one (see Table 6) but Trudgill's final remark, in parentheses, applies to all children whose speech contains features of Creole and those who choose to deepen them in some contexts. We know from the experience in Trinidad that the attempt to make Creole acceptable in school meets with the most vehement opposition even, perhaps especially, in its native home. However, what is at stake here is much more than merely tolerating the dialect of the pupil. For many pupils speaking the dialect means saying something uniquely. It may mean more. The very act of speaking it is a declaration of who and what they are and wish to be. Furthermore, West Indian dialect speakers are heirs to an almost exclusively oral tradition (we shall qualify this later). Their stories, verbal wit and songs are a popular aesthetic resource which should not be shut out by teachers who would be the first to claim that they are centrally concerned with imagination, authenticity and the creative use of language.

It is difficult to develop a sane policy on these matters, avoiding on the one hand preservationist enthusiasms not shared by the pupils, and on the other steadfast blindness to the significance of black speech for some pupils, especially those who choose to switch at times from a form of British English to London Jamaican. There are teachers who can develop styles of work which emerge productively from the dilemma:

> Elaine's sister Judith had told something like eight or nine Anansi stories on tape — some of which we made into booklets — before it occurred to me that we could lend her a tape-recorder and ask her to record her mother. This she did. Her mother an 'ordinary' working class woman is as fine a story-teller as anyone anywhere. You don't have to go to the Brothers Grimm, or this or that Book of Beautiful Tales. Great story tellers are amongst us. Sometimes we call them parents. If you have some of these stories on tape, what happens? The parents' culture becomes part of the curriculum. . .
> (Rosen, M, 1978)

Other initiatives are reported in Edwards (1979), Chapter 6, and we have already shown (Section 7 of this chapter) how the study of linguistic diversity can make its contribution. Sutcliffe (1976, 1978) has given us an outstanding description and documentation of the creativity of West Indian children's speech in England.

Reading and dialect

It is often argued that dialect is a serious handicap to the learning of reading and, of course, that West Indian pupils are more handicapped than other dialect speakers. Reading is in the limelight of current educational debate and there are very different views about how it should be taught. That confrontation is too huge to be assessed here. We shall instead offer Goodman's change of view which can be examined in more detail by those who have doubts. In 1965, Goodman argued that the greater the linguistic distance the more the reading process is hampered. By 1973 (Goodman and Buck) he had completely changed his position. Since he is the chief exponent of the school which argues that 'translation' by the learner-reader is a mark of real progress, this is scarcely to be wondered at. A dialect synonym or analogous structure offered instead of the words on the page indicates reading for meaning whereas a word-for-word correct reading may conceal failure to grasp meaning. Goodman finally saw it this way:

> The only disadvantage which speakers of low-status dialects suffer in learning to read is imposed by teachers and schools. Rejection of their dialects and educators' confusion of linguistic difference with linguistic deficiency interferes with the natural process by which language is acquired and undermines the linguistic confidence of divergent speakers.

The onus is here placed firmly on the teachers, not only to adopt a positive attitude to dialect, but also to make sufficient effort to learn about the features of dialect to avoid confusing children. Labov (1972a) shows in considerable detail how such confusion can be created but his final conclusion is that this is not the major cause of difficulty which is, rather, that reading failure arises from the rejection of school culture. This may well be true of New York black children but it would be unwise to assume a similar attitude in Britain by large numbers of young vernacular speakers. Our attention should be focused on the kinds of correction insisted on by teachers, since these are often attempts to change the speech of the children as though this were an essential part of the process of learning to read. It needs to be reiterated that of the varied ways of pronouncing, let us say, the word 'bank' in English no one way is the correct reading.

We think that one of the most promising developments in reading in a multilinguistic setting is the material developed at the Centre for Urban Educational Studies (Wight *et al*, 1978). In the Teachers Notes to *Make-a-Story* a section is devoted to dialect and it ends with these comments:

> In preparing these materials we also carried out some investigations into dialect in the infant classroom. We wanted to know whether there were important dialect differences in the classroom English of black and white five-year-olds in order to examine the theory that such differences might interfere with the process of learning to read. We found fewer differences than anticipated. The majority (four-fifths) of the West Indian children displayed the same sort of grammatical usage as their white peers. And the speech of the remaining fifth was not dramatically different. It did not appear on the basis of this evidence that dialect variation between the child's classroom speech and the text in early reading books should create difficulties of understanding for the child. (This is not to say that there is always a satisfactory match between the English of some early reading materials — 'readerese' — and the speech of young children. The discrepancy, however, is *not* dialect based.)
>
> Although the child's home dialect will not make early reading material unintelligible, it may still have an impact on the way he learns to read. Whether it interferes or not will depend on the teacher's understanding of the child's dialect and his/her policy on correcting children's early reading.

The writing of dialect and Standard
The significance of the printed and written language for the dialect speakers is quite different from reading. The printed

language is almost entirely Standard. To learn to read is to learn to read Standard. This has never meant that in order to read, dialect speakers had to learn to speak Standard. Millions of regional speakers are avid readers of newspapers written entirely in Standard. There is one important exception to the universality of Standard, namely printed literature in the artistic sense of that term. There is a long tradition of dialect literature in England. During the nineteenth century it flourished in the North of England. It is a common practice for novelists, poets and playwrights to introduce dialect through dialogue. But since Standard now completely dominates writing, the writing of dialect soon puts a writer in difficulties. There are no widely accepted orthographic conventions. Where such conventions exist, in the absence of common familiarity, the reader is plunged into a taxing deciphering exercise. Any attempt to be faithful to dialect phonology enforces compromises. The paradox is, therefore, that dialect speakers may find it more difficult to read attempts at written forms of their own dialect than Standard. The writing of Standard, therefore, becomes an acceptable and essential goal in a way which the speaking of Standard does not. There are major changes which all speakers have to make when moving from speech to writing though some may have to make more than others.

We are certainly not suggesting that all written English needs to be in Standard and that dialect writing should be outlawed. On the contrary, we would propose that there is a special place for dialect writing as there always has been, that is in the literature created by pupils — stories, poems, plays and expressive writing generally. Where there is a dialect literature growing up (as there is for the West Indian community)* there is the advantage of an adult literate culture to draw upon. It has been argued that dialect writing can help in the writing of Standard since it is likely to sharpen perception of differences.

However, dialect in the written language is not simply a choice between permitting it or suppressing it. Dialects infiltrate into attempts to write Standard. We would argue that although every effort should be made to help in the confident mastery of the Standard written language, there should be less anxiety about the relatively few dialect forms which young writers

*We made the reluctant decision not to include in this chapter a discussion of the implications of linguistic diversity for the literature curriculum. It goes without saying that they are profound but we felt they defied cursory treatment and were of a more narrowly specialist interest than the rest of the chapter.

135

introduce into their work. Finally, it should be remembered that the written language operates at different levels of formality. At its most informal it comes closer to the spoken language when dialect can enter more appropriately than Standard.

Since we have accepted that learning to write Standard must be a goal for all pupils, we conclude that a profound examination of what this process involves for different kinds of dialect speakers needs to be undertaken, in particular how the composing process can be mediated by teachers and pupils and bridges built between spoken and written models.

10 ENGLISH AS A SECOND LANGUAGE

We might well have made no comment on 'ESL' on the grounds that this is a highly developed curriculum area with its own literature and specialists. We shall make no attempt to survey those resources. However, as our figures and discussion make clear, there are questions which of necessity take us into terrain which cannot be divided by a neat frontier into English-as-a-second-language and English-as-a-first-language. In the first place, there are many children who begin with the first and have ended with the second. Secondly, there is no clear cut-off point at which we can say that a pupil is ready to join an English-medium class and will cope with learning as well as an English-as-a-first-language child. The whole operation becomes more hazardous if that child is left to sink or swim. If he is sinking, there is a better chance that rescue attempts will be made than if efforts to swim look reasonably convincing. There is abundant evidence to show that the pupils who are most easily 'lost' are those whose knowledge of English is amply sufficient for daily communicative needs, including many which arise in the classroom, but who meet serious difficulty when faced with the textbook language and, teachers' exposition and the language of literature. Subtleties of tone and style can easily elude them. A recent ILEA survey of primary and secondary schools showed that approximately 42 per cent of children with another language were identified as 'needing help with English' and that nearly half the classes have between one and nine pupils in the category. For a small, but not insignificant minority, classroom language is not intelligible. For them undoubtedly the best tried methods of ESL teaching should be available but for the majority what is needed is a *school policy of support in the normal classroom.*

We therefore suggest that:

(i) schools should identify those pupils in need of support and should take care not to omit needs of those who are at later stages of mastery of English

(ii) ESL and English ('mother tongue') teachers should work in close collaboration. The transition to the normal classroom should not mean the abandonment of specialist support. Separate organization of the two kinds of teachers is probably counter-productive.

(iii) in-service programmes should include the study by teachers of the 'interlanguage' of their pupils.

The English language learners encounter many kinds of English, spoken and written, and the 'target' language changes under their very eyes, e.g. peer group English, teachers' English, written Standard English, the interlanguage of others like themselves. It may be necessary to make explicit differences which are relatively self-evident to native speakers.

In spite of all we have said, we should remember all those children who, given reasonably favourable school circumstances, become very effective users of the English language. It is the creation of those circumstances which is the major task.

10   LANGUAGE ACROSS THE CURRICULUM

For more than ten years the authors of this report have been involved in initiating and developing the programmatic concept of language across the curriculum and we have seen no reason to change the basic propositions outlined in *Language, the Learner and the School* (Barnes *et al*, 1971) and developed in later work. We have always been conscious of the need to carry forward the detailed application of those ideas. The experience we have now accumulated in inner-city schools including the carrying out of the survey reported here, has persuaded us that we now need to adapt and enrich our views.

There is a growing understanding that the language children are expected to *receive* in school is often opaque and mystifying and that their learning is hampered accordingly. It faces them in textbooks, worksheets, exercises, examinations and often the teachers' exposition. What should at its best be a liberating experience becomes an imprisoning one. There is often an alarming gap yawning between the language which pupils are expected to comprehend and the language which they bring to school. This takes on new meaning when we consider the range of language repertoires in the classroom and the different ways in which the values, attitudes and concepts are expressed in different cultures. Some of the difficulties arise because the language put before them is inappropriate. It makes assumptions about them as readers and listeners which take no account of their ways of understanding and their language resources. The experienced reader/listener often has similar difficulties and overcomes them by active internal dialogue but many pupils need to have texts mediated for them in discussion with the teacher and with fellow-pupils. In this way the gap can be bridged. Children should not be left to pore uncomprehendingly over texts, left with a sense of failure and defeat. When English is a second language the failure and defeat are more total.

To suggest that more discussion and talk of all kinds is a necessity is to repeat, yet again, one of the main language-across-the-curriculum proposals. It takes on a new dimension if we remember that some pupils will be learning English in this way and practising it in ways which teacher recitation or interrogation cannot encompass. All pupils can extend their language into new areas of experience and understanding offered by the curriculum by actively formulating for themselves new ideas and opinions.

But this is more complicated than we might once have thought: communicative patterns, the ways in which the spoken language is used, may vary in dramatic ways. What are the 'rules' for when you speak and when you stay silent and when and how you may interrupt? Differences in ways of talking may be more important than differences between languages more narrowly conceived. It may be that we have asked for more talk in the classroom. We have asked for *one* way, our way. As Hymes (1972) puts it:

> Those brought together in classrooms, even though having the language of the classroom in common, may not be wholly members of the same speech communities.

This suggests that children need to come to terms through their interaction with each other's ways of talking rather than conform to the one pattern of listen-and-answer. We have to learn more about the variations of speech style of different groups. The facts of linguistic diversity should oblige us to do something we might well have started on before. We have learnt a lot from the description by Labov and others of black youngsters' verbal play. Who has done the same for Cockney children's skill at repartee and having the last word?

There is a tension set up in schools betwen learning to say it the teachers' way (or write it the teachers' way) and finding your own way of saying it. That oversimplifies the choice deliberately and unashamedly because there is so much empty imitation which is accepted as learning and relatively little encouragement of the pupils' efforts and struggles to express observations, ideas and conclusions in the language available to them. Linguistic diversity proposes to us that we should find a very wide range of expression as acceptable as evidence of effective learning. The old obsessions with a very narrowly conceived set of acceptable conventions become even more unhelpful.

All schools explicitly and implicitly convey to their pupils their expectations in language as well as other matters. They need to find ways of showing through their practices that diversity is not Babel and that they can combine an appreciation of the pupils' languages and dialects with bold ambitions to add to their communicative and expressive power.

There is a sour joke amongst readers of research reports that the main conclusion of most research is that more research should be done. We have dropped marker buoys in our text to indicate how we hope this study will be followed by others which will change some of our misty speculations into well-lit lucidities. We have also made a start ourselves. There is a lot to do. Our preference would be for research energy to be directed above all to the consequences of linguistic diversity for classrooms but that programme needs itself to be sustained by thorough sociolinguistic descriptions which could be shaped as instruments for teachers as well as contributing to scholarly literature.

We had almost forgotten the poser with which we started this chapter. It was from the teacher who wanted to know what difference it all makes to the way you teach $2 + 2 = 4$. From one point of view the answer is, none at all. The accommodation of linguistic and cultural diversity calls for a change in how we perceive children so that school is seen by them as a place which is theirs. Yet there are many ways of teaching $2 + 2 = 4$. What comes in twos in one culture may be different from what comes in twos in another. The necessary mathematical understanding cannot be derived from reiteration of or contemplation of the figures. Talk has to come into it somewhere and experience too. But that fragment of learning has to be fitted into the construction of the whole edifice of multi-cultural education. In constructing it some of our most cherished practices will need to be revised. In the process all pupils, speakers of all kinds, should be the beneficiaries, even though some of them were not being thought of when newly-arrived languages and dialects obliged us to take a closer look at the resources of all children and consider how those resources fare in the school system.

Indeed since the beginnings of stratified society and the use of writing, it has been characteristic of the greater part of mankind that a desired or required communicative competence has confronted man as an alien thing, imposed by a power not within his control. In the complex circumstances of our own society it is hard to see how children can be expected to master a second system, complementing or replacing their own, if the process is not perceived as intrinsically relevant or enjoyable, preferably both.

(D. Hymes, 1971b)

Bibliography

ALATIS, J. E. (ed) (1978) *International Dimensions of Bilingual Education* George Town University

ANSRE, G. (1975) 'Madina: three polygots and some implications for Ghana' in Ohanessian *et al* (1975)

BARNES, D., BRITTON, J., and ROSEN, H. (Rev. edn 1971) *Language, the Learner and the School* Penguin

BELL, R. T. (1976) *Sociolinguistics* Batsford

BICKERTON, D. (1975) *The Dynamics of a Creole System* CUP

BOURHIS, R. Y. and GILES, H. (1977) 'The language of intergroup distinctiveness' in Giles, H. (ed) (1972)

CAMPBELL-PLATT, K. (1976) 'Distribution of linguistic minorities in Britain' in *Bilingualism and British Education* CILT 1976

CAMPBELL-PLATT, K. (1978) *Linguistic Minorities in Britain* Runnymede Trust

CANDLIN, C. and DERRICK, J. (2nd edition 1973) *Language* Commission for Racial Equality

CHILD, I. L. (1943) *Italian or American? The Second Generation in Conflict* Yale University

CILT (Centre for Information in Language Teaching) (1976) *Bilingualism and British Education*

CLAYDON, L., KNIGHT, T. and RADO, M. (1977) *Curriculum and Culture: Schooling in a Pluralist Society* Allen and Unwin (Australia)

CROSS, C. (1978) *Ethnic Minorities in the Inner City* Commission for Racial Equality

DERRICK, J. (1966) *Teaching English to Immigrants* Longman

DERRICK, J. (1977) *The Language Needs of Minority Group Children* NFER

DES (1975) *A Language for Life* The Bullock Report HMSO

EDWARDS, A. D. (1976) *Language in Culture and Class* Heinemann Educational

EDWARDS, V. K. (1976) 'Effects of dialect on the comprehension of West Indian children' *Educational Research*, 18: pp. 83—95

EDWARDS, V. K. (1979) *The West Indian Language Issue in British Schools* Routledge and Kegan Paul

EPSTEIN, N. (1977) *Language, Ethnicity and the Schools* George Washington University

FERGUSON, C. A. (1966) 'National sociolinguistic profile formulas' in Bright, W. (ed) *Sociolinguistics* Mouton

FISHMAN, J. (1971) 'National languages and languages of wider communication' in Whiteley, W. H., *Language Use and Social Change* OUP

FISHMAN, J. A. (1977) 'Language and ethnicity' in Giles, H. (ed) (1977)

GILES, H. (ed) (1977) *Language, Ethnicity, and Intergroup Relations* Academic Press

GILES, H., BOURHIS, R. Y. and TAYLOR, D. M. (1977) 'Towards a theory of language in ethnic group relations' in Giles, H. (1977)

GILES, H. and POWESLAND, P. F. (1975) *Speech Style and Social Evaluation* Academic Press

GOODMAN, K. S. and BUCK, C. (1973) 'Dialect barriers to reading comprehension revisited' in *The Reading Teacher*, Vol. 27, No. 1, pp. 6–12

GREENBERG, J. H. (1956) 'The measurement of linguistic diversity' *Language*, 32

GREGORY, M. and CARROLL, S. (1978) *Language and Situation* Routledge and Kegan Paul

GUMPERZ, J. (1968) 'The speech community' in *International Encyclopaedia of the Social Sciences* Macmillan

GUMPERZ, J. and HYMES, D. (eds) (1972) *Directions in Sociolinguistics* Holt, Rinehart and Winston

HALLIDAY, M. A. K. (1978) *Language as Social Semoitic* Arnold

HAUGEN, E. (1973) 'The curse of Babel', *Daedalus*, Vol. 102, No. 3

HEBIDGE, D. (1976) 'Reggae, rastas and rudies' in Hall, S. and Jefferson, T. (eds) *Youth Subcultures in Post-war Britain* Hutchinson

HMSO (1963) *English for Immigrants, Education Pamphlet 43*

HMSO (1972) *The Continuing Needs of Immigrants, Education Survey 14*

HMSO (1971) *The Education of Immigrants, Education Survey 13*

HORNBY, P. A. (ed) (1977) *Bilingualism: Psychological, Social and Educational Implications* Academic Press

HYMES, D. (1971a) 'On communicative competence' in Pride, J. B. and Holmes, J. (eds) (1972) *Sociolinguistics*, Penguin

HYMES, D. (1971b) 'Competence and performance in linguistic theory' in Huxley, R. and Ingram, E. *Language Acquisition: Models and Methods*, Academic Press

HYMES, D. (1972) Introduction to Cazden, C., John, V. and Hymes, D. *Functions of Language in the Classroom*, Teachers College Press, Columbia University

JEFFCOATE, R. (1979) *Positive Image: Towards a Multiracial Curriculum* Chameleon

KHAN, V. S. (1976) 'Provision by minorities for language maintenance' in *Bilingualism and British Education* CILT 1976

KHAN, V. S. (1978) *Bilingualism and Minority Languages in Britain* Runnymede Trust

KHAN, V. S. (ed) (1979) *Minority Families in Britain* Macmillan

KRANZ, E. (1971) *Ethnic Minorities in Britain* Paladin

LABOV, W. (ed) (1972a) *Language in the Inner City* University of Pennsylvania

LABOV, W. (1972b) *Sociolinguistic Patterns* University of Pennsylvania

LAMBERT, W. E. (1977) 'The effects of bilingualism on the individual: cognitive and social consequences' in Hornby, E. (ed) (1977)

LEWIS, E. G. (1970) 'Immigrants: their languages and development', in *Trends in Education*, 19, 1970

LIEBERSON, S. (1964) 'An extension of Greenberg's linguistic diversity measures', *Language*, **40**

LOCKWOOD, W. B. (1975) *Languages of the British Isles, Past and Present*

MACNAMARA, J. (1966) *Bilingualism and Primary Education* Edinburgh University Press

OHANNESSIAN, S., FERGUSON, C. A. and POLOME, E. C. (eds) (1975) *Language Surveys in Developing Nations* Centre for Applied Linguistics, Arlington

ORTON, H., SANDERSON M and WIDDOWSON M (1978) *Linguistic Atlas of England* Croom Helm

ORTON, H. and WRIGHT, N. (1974) *A Word Geography of England* Seminar Press

PARKIN, D. 'Emergent and stabilized multilingualism: peer-groups in urban Kenya' in Giles, H. (ed) (1977)

PARLIAMENT OF THE COMMONWEALTH OF AUSTRALIA (1975) *Report of the enquiry into schools of high migrant density* Parliamentary Paper No. 300

PERREN, G. E. (1979) 'Languages and minority groups' in Perren, G. E. (ed) *The Mother Tongue and other Languages in Education*, CILT

RICHARDS, J. C. (1974) *Error Analysis: Perspectives on Second Language Acquisition* Newbury House

RICHARDS, J. C. (ed) (1978) *Understanding Second and Foreign Language Learning* Newbury House

ROSEN, H. (1979) 'Dialect diversity and education' in *Dialekt og rikssprak i skulun* Universitet 1 Oslo

ROSEN, M. (1978) 'In their own voice', *Issues in Race and Education*, No.16

SANKOFF, D. (ed) (1978) *Linguistic Variation: Models and Methods*

SHUY, R. W. and FASOLD, R. W. (eds) (1976) *Language Attitudes: Current Trends and Prospects* George Town University

SHARP, D. (1973) *Language in Bilingual Communities* Arnold

SHARP, D. *et al* (1973) *Attitudes to Welsh and English in the Schools of Wales* University of Wales

SIMOES, A. (1976) *The Bilingual Child* Academic Press

SMITH, D. M. and SHUY, R. W. (eds) (1972) *Sociolinguistics in Cross-cultural Analysis* Georgetown University

SPOLSKY, B. (ed) (1972) *The Language Education of Minority Children* Newbury House

STEPHENS, M. (1976) *Linguistic Minorities in Western Europe* Gomer Press

STEWART, W. A. (1968) 'A sociolinguistic typology for describing multi-lingualism' in Fishman, J. *Readings in the Sociology of Language*, Mouton

SUTCLIFFE, D. (1976) 'Hou dem taak in Bedford, Sa' in *Multiracial School*, Vol. 5, No. 1, pp. 19—24

SUTCLIFFE, D. (1978) *The language of first and second generation of West Indian children in Bedfordshire*, unpublished M. Ed. thesis, University of Leicester

TOSI, A. (1979) 'Semilingualism, diglossia and bilingualism: some observations on the sociolinguistic features of a community of Southern

Italians in Britain', *Lingua e Contesto*, No. 4, Manfredonia: Atlantica
TRUDGILL, P. J. (1974) *The Social Differentiation of English in Norwich* CUP
TRUDGILL, P. J. (1975) *Accent, Dialect and the School* Arnold
TRUDGILL, P. J. (1978) *Sociolinguistic Patterns in British English* Arnold
TRUDGILL, P. J. (1979) 'Standard and non-Standard dialects of English in the United Kingdom: problems and policies', *Intl. J. Soc. Lang.* 21 (1979), pp. 9—24
WAKELIN, M. (1978) *Discovering English Dialects* Shire Publications
WATSON, J. L. (ed) (1979) *Between Two Cultures* Blackwell
WEINREICH, U. (1953) *Languages in Contact* Mouton
WELLS, J. C. (1973) *Jamaican Pronunciation in London* Blackwell
WIGHT, J., HUNT, P., SAPARA, S. and SINCLAIR, H. (1978)
  — *Explore-a-story* (Collins and ILEA)
  — *Share-a-story* (Holmes McDougall and ILEA)
  — *Make-a-story* (Holmes McDougall and ILEA)
WILLIAMS, F. (ed) (1970) *Language and Poverty* Markham
WRIGHT, J. 'Bilingualism and schooling in multilingual Britain', *Junction*, Summer 1978

Appendix 1

UNIVERSITY OF LONDON
INSTITUTE OF EDUCATION
DEPARTMENT OF TEACHING OF
ENGLISH

SURVEY OF LINGUISTIC DIVERSITY IN ILEA SECONDARY SCHOOLS

Introduction to questionnaire

Research Director: Harold Rosen
Research Officer: Tony Burgess
Research Secretary: Antoinette Pernetta
English Dept., Institute of Education,
20, Bedford Way, London WC1
(tel. 01-636 1500)

SURVEY OF LINGUISTIC DIVERSITY IN ILEA SECONDARY SCHOOLS

Introduction

The aim behind the questions which follow is really very straight-forward: to make an estimate of the extent of linguistic diversity in ILEA secondary schools. Our central question is 'Who speaks which language or dialect?' At present, no systematised information about this question is available. So the document in front of you, which we are asking you and your colleagues to complete for all first year pupils in your school, is a first step towards building up a picture of the language situation.

We are grateful for your help. In return, may we promise — to you as to all schools contributing to this survey:

(1) that the information collected in your school will be made available to you, just as soon as we have analysed it;

AND

(2) that as and when an overall picture for the ILEA emerges, you will be the first to know.

This is the least that we could promise, we are aware. We do have some hope, though, that this document could be a talking point for staff interested in language and that the act of filling it in may be of use to you in thinking about language diversity in the classes you teach and in the school as a whole.

Linguistic diversity

A word of introduction about language diversity and what we mean by it. Our starting assumption is that the linguistic situation in inner London is relatively complex — more complex (say) than in a rural area. Greater heterogeneity of language may be present even there than is often recognised. In inner London, though, as in other large centres of population, the situation is qualitatively different. A large number of different languages and of different dialects of the same language exist side by side. Our classrooms reflect this situation and it is this, very generally, that we wish to map.

146

Reasons for the survey

Our reasons are educational rather than linguistic. A number of hypotheses link language with educational achievement, as you will know. It is not our intention in this survey to emerge with some final adjudication between them. The plain fact is that very little is known about the scale on which different languages and dialects are spoken by pupils in our schools — either in London or elsewhere. Such knowledge could contribute, we believe, to a more informed practice.

That puts it very generally. There are, as well, some more clear cut directions which evidence from this survey will touch. Thus, from your answers to the questions which follow, we hope we may be able to:

(1) Make an estimate of the scale and significance of both Great Britain and overseas based dialects of English — and of languages other than English — in considering the language demands of secondary education.
(2) Make an estimate of the scale and significance of non-standard dialects of English — and of languages other than English — in the acquisition of literacy in Standard English.
(3) Make an estimate of the scale and significance of the numbers of pupils at an intermediate stage in the acquisition of English as a second language.
(4) Collect information relevant to the maintenance of languages other than English in inner London schools.

We hope this makes our intentions plain — and also the kind of use to which the information will be put.

Nevertheless, there are one or two points which should be added here. May we stress that our focus is on language not country of origin and that our interest is in general trends not specific pupils. The anonymity of pupils will be preserved, as we explain later. We also recognise the right of individual pupils (and teachers) to decline to be involved in the survey. In instances of this kind we ask that a nil return be entered on the questionnaires for the pupil(s) affected.

Naturally we should regret the gap in our information that this will entail. But we respect the right to such a decision.

Support in filling in the questionnaire

So the simple question in this document (Who speaks what?) leads, as you will see, to a number of others. Probably it all looks so formidable that you may be discouraged. But it is neither as complicated nor as demanding as it seems at first sight. For instance, there seem to be many questions and alternatives — the result of having to allow for many different types of speaker. However, you will find that somewhere between 4–10 questions suffice for any single pupil.

Nowhere, either, are we looking for honed, linguistic descriptions, but for your judgement as a teacher about the language of the pupils you teach — on the basis, almost entirely, of your everyday, professional knowledge about them.

Probably more important than either of these reassurances is the fact that we will do our utmost to ease the chore in the demands which we are making. As a first principle: no school will be asked to work on these questionnaires without accompanying support — someone from the project who will visit the school a number of times to help with completing the questions and to advise about difficulties. A further point about this. If you have not been personally contacted already, you will be very soon. Please do nothing about the questionnaires until someone from the project visits. It will be best if we can work through any problems together.

In the end we are very reliant on your good will and your judgement. This we know and appreciate.

Terms and definitions
Languages

The terms, here and in the questions which follow, need clarifying. Forgive us if we seem to be explaining the obvious. In the language diversity in schools the most striking differences are those between distinct languages (e.g. English, Gujerati, Greek etc.). One language differs from others because it has a relatively independent grammatical system, sound system and vocabulary. Languages also differ because they are expressions of marked differences of cultural and national identity. Of course there is no simple equivalence between language and country of origin. There is no language 'African' or 'Indian' — or for that matter British. Different languages (e.g. English) may cross national, cultural and geographical boundaries and, at the same time, within any one set of these boundaries, it is often the case that many different languages are spoken (e.g. in India, Gujerati, Hindi, Bengali, Urdu and others).

Dialects
Now, a further point. The presence of pupils speaking different languages, perhaps as their mother tongue, is only one aspect of the linguistic diversity to be found in many inner London classrooms. There are also significant *differences of dialect*. Such differences, in any language, can also relate to national and cultural boundaries (e.g. variants of English in Africa, West Indies, America, Great Britain); to different geographical regions within countries (e.g. variants of English in London, Yorkshire, Northumberland etc.); and to differences of social class (e.g. Working class, Middle class).

Dialects are variations within a single language. These variations are systematic and relatively permanent. A dialect may be located within geographical, national or social boundaries. A dialect will have distinctive features such as accent, idioms (turns of phrase), intonation (patterns of rise and fall in the speech), syntax (grammatical constructions) etc.

Dialects of English
So much for dialect in general. What about *dialects of English* specifically? In many inner London classrooms there will be some pupils who speak a Great Britain based dialect of English (from within the London area and, to a lesser extent, some originating outside it) and some who speak an overseas based dialect of English (e.g. different Caribbean dialects of English, American, Australian dialects of English etc.).

There will also be *social* dialect differences. This applies both to Great Britain based and overseas based dialects. The distinction in Great Britain is between what is basically called *Standard English* (the dialect which is accorded cultural dominance) and other dialects both regional and social. Similar distinctions exist within overseas dialects of English (e.g. for the Caribbean, between the Standard of a particular region or island — Jamaican Standard — and the non-standard, local form Jamaican creole).

The range of diversity
Languages and dialects, then — these are the components of the diversity we are interested in. It may help to set out the total pattern diagrammatically.

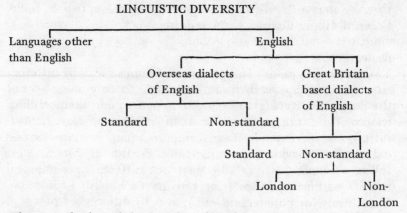

LINGUISTIC DIVERSITY

Languages other than English

English

Overseas dialects of English

Great Britain based dialects of English

Standard   Non-standard

Standard   Non-standard

London   Non-London

The complexity of the London situation

This diagram sets out the total range of possibilities. But there is one very important qualification to be made about it. As a model, it separates out kinds of language. In the classrooms the distinctions will not be so clear cut. Deciding on the language background will be straightforward enough for some pupils: most speakers of a Great Britain based dialect of English (Standard, London, non-London). With others it will not be so simple. For example, West Indian pupils, many of them born in this country, will often be predominantly speakers of a Great Britain based dialect of English, but will also often incorporate into their speech some features from a Caribbean Standard or non-standard English. A number of pupils will be multi-dialectal or multi-lingual. And so on.

Detailed notes about such problems of deciding on the speech of the pupil are given in the introductions to the two alternative sections of the questionnaire. Enough to say here that the picture is a blurred and complicated one. The complexity of the situation is of course precisely the issue which we are interested in.

Filling in the questionnaire:
General introductory notes

Note 1: Organisation of the questionnaire

The basis is the individual pupil. We are asking you and your colleagues, then, to complete a set of the accompanying questions for each pupil in each class or group of the first year pupils in your school.

Note 2: General pupil information
We should be grateful for a few details of general information about the pupil, before you begin. May we ask you to enter this on the page before the main body of the questions.

What we are asking for here should be largely self-explanatory. The pupil code-number, however, needs a word of explanation. We should like to adopt a system for distinguishing between different pupils which allows for two things: (a) for the pupil's anonymity to be preserved and (b) for particular pupils to be traceable, if necessary, through you.

We ask you, then, to enter for the pupil a code number only. This we will determine when we visit the school. However, we should also be grateful if you would preserve a record of the allocation of numbers to pupils. This would both make it possible to trace different pupils should we need to, but also ensure that it can only be done with your permission. We can discuss this further when we visit.

Note 3: Alternative sections (A or B)
The questions are organised in two sections, with parallel subdivisions in each section. These two principal sections are alternatives.

Section A: for pupils who speak a Great Britain based dialect of English (Standard, London or Non-London) and whose speech incorporates NO features which derive either from an overseas dialect of English (e.g. Caribbean, Australian) or from a language other than English (e.g. Greek, Gujerati).

OR

Section B: for pupils in the process of learning English as a second language (at whatever stage) or, more generally, whose speaking of English DOES incorporate features from an overseas dialect of English or from a language other than English. This very broad grouping is, of course, further sub-divided within the section.

More detailed guidance about the bases on which to allocate pupils to one section rather than the other follows in the introductory notes to the sections themselves. At this point,

151

please simply note:

- that the two sections are alternatives and that for any one pupil either section A or section B should be completed only. The alternative section should simply be omitted.
- that in cases of doubt about whether the English speech of some pupils does in fact incorporate some overseas features, and where an overseas background is known, it will usually be more convenient to use section B. Subsequent questions in that section will help you to clarify the situation.

Note 4: Sub-divisions in Sections A and B
Both Section A and Section B are sub-divided into three parallel parts, as follows:

SECTION A:
Part A.1:   Which Great Britain based dialect of English?
Part A.2:   Reading and Writing
Part A.3:   Any overseas based dialect of or language other than English?
SECTION B:
Part B.1:   Which overseas dialect of English OR which language other than English?
Part B.2:   Reading and Writing
Part B.3:   Any (or any further) overseas based dialect or language other than English?

There is also an optional part 4 to both sections in which we should be grateful for any additional comments which you or your pupil may be able to make.

There are also further sub-sections to part 1 and 3 of both Section A and Section B. It is not necessary to list these here. Broadly they are alternatives within the main theme of the part, introduced to allow for economy in reading and answering the questions. Only those sub-sections which are applicable to any particular pupil should be completed. Others can simply be omitted.

Again, more detailed guidance is given in the introductory notes to Section A and Section B. At this stage please simply note that we ask you to complete all three parts of either

Section A or Section B.

Note 5: Additional comments — from you and/or your pupils
Most of the accompanying questions take the form of asking
you to indicate the most accurate among several possibilities.
Space is left in each part for additional comment and we should
be grateful for anything you can provide. In some, though not
all, questions, we have alllowed for the indication, on your part,
of further possibilities than we may have envisaged.

Finally, in part 4 of each of the two major sections, we have
left room for any additional comment of a more general nature.
We are particularly interested in any light which might be
thrown on the way the pupil's language has changed over the
past few years and how he/she perceives this change. This we
could not explore explicitly in the questionnaire. Needless to
say, this section is strictly optional. But your answers here
could help us a lot.

SECTION A: A GREAT BRITAIN BASED DIALECT OF ENGLISH

Note 1: Choice of section A or section B
If you have chosen to allocate the pupil to section A, you will
have been guided, we envisage, by two considerations:

(a)   *the pupil speaks a Great Britain based dialect of English,
      either*
              — London or
              *— a dialect of a region in Great Britain outside London,
              or*
              — Standard English;
AND
(b)   the pupil's speech incorporates NO features deriving from
      an overseas dialect of English (e.g. Jamaican creole) or a
      language other than English (e.g. Gujerati) — nor is it
      marked by inexperience with English constructions.

A word of explanation about this second criterion. Remember
that the focus is on language, not on the pupil's country of
origin. We should expect that some pupils of overseas origin
should be allocated to this section; for they may be speakers of

153

a Great Britain based dialect of English, which is entirely uninfluenced by features deriving from an overseas dialect or language.

If in doubt whether the pupil is in this category, allocate him/her to section B. This need not mean that in your view the pupil is an inexperienced speaker of English. It will be the case with some of the pupils allocated to section B, but not with all. Many may well be experienced speakers of English — and, what is more, effective ones. The principle in question concerns the features and influences in the pupil's speech.

Note 2: How the section is organised
The section is in three parts, as follows:
Part A.1:   *Which Great Britain based dialect of English does the pupil speak?*
Part A.2:   *How fluent and independent is the pupil as a Reader and Writer?*
Part A.3:   *Does the pupil speak, in addition, a language other than English or an overseas dialect of English.*

We have separated the parts for the convenience of filling in. Each of these parts, however, contains no more than one or two questions.

Note 3: Choice of dialect (Part A.1)
In part 1 of this section we are concerned with the question: *'Which Great Britain based dialect of English?'* Don't worry if your answer is based on a relatively rough and ready judgement. 'London', one of the choices we offer, is clearly a pretty broad category and refers not to a single speech but to a continuum. Differences between dialects, anyway, are those of a continuum and are not absolute. So precise specification is not expected.

Note 4: Strength of dialectal features (Q1, Q3, Q4)
Similar considerations apply to our further question: *'How would you estimate the strength of the dialectal features?'* We are asking for a rough judgement only, based on an impression which will be the product of several interwoven features. We have itemised some of these, such as idioms (turns of phrase), accent, intonation (patterns in the speech's rise and fall), syntax (grammatical constructions), style. But they are not often heard as distinct, separate features. We are asking for

a judgement formed on your impressions.

Note 5: Reading and writing (Part A.2)
In part 2 of the section, we ask you to make a rough estimate of the *pupil's competence as a reader and writer.* Again we are looking for your best, rough estimate only. If none of these three options fit, please feel free to add you own comment.

Note 6: Other languages or dialects (Part A.3)
In the third, formal part of the section, we are interested in *any other languages or dialect which the pupil may speak.* This will apply to some pupils only and is anyway supplementary information to that which you will already have given. Some pupils, though, may also speak an overseas dialect of English or a language other than English (apart of course from school taught 'modern languages': we don't mean these). We should be grateful for information of this kind.

Our principal concern here is with *'the extent of use' (Q10, Q14).* A word about this and about bilingualism (and bi-dialectalism), in particular. Specialisation of language for particular contexts is the usual form for bilingualism to take. So the fact that a pupil may use a language other than English only for (e.g.) talking to his parents would not be a reason for denying bilingual status. It is unlikely that a pupil for whom a language other than English was his/her dominant language should have been appropriately allocated to this section. But it is just conceivable and hence we offer this possibility as well.

Finally, *reading and writing in the language other than English (Q11, Q15).* We realise in this and probably in other questions in this part you will have to rely heavily on your judgement of the pupil and on information you gather from him/her. Please do the best you can.

Note 7: Part A.4
This will be self-explanatory. We'd be very grateful for anything you can offer — or your pupil if you think it appropriate.

SECTION B: AN OVERSEAS DIALECT OF ENGLISH, OR A LANGUAGE OTHER THAN ENGLISH

Introductory notes

Note 1: Choice of section B or section A
If you have chosen to allocate the pupil to section B, you will have had in mind, we envisage, someone who conforms to one of the following (very loose) specifications:

(a) *a pupil in the process of learning English as a second language (at whatever stage), whose first language (mother tongue) was a language other than English;*

OR

(b) *a pupil (probably but not necessarily a recent arrival in Great Britain) whose speech is predominantly that of an overseas based dialect of English (e.g. a Caribbean standard or creole, American, Australian Standard or local regional dialect etc.);*

OR

(c) *a pupil, who may well be a highly experienced and effective speaker of one of the Great Britain based dialects of English (London, Non-London, Standard), but whose speech incorporates, or is influenced by, some other features — features which derive either from a language other than English or from an overseas dialect of English.*

In allocating a pupil to section B, then, we are asking you to concentrate first on the pupil as a speaker of English. Your estimate of this, of the features and influences in the pupil's English speech, contains the central principle of allocation.

One more word about the pupils whom we have roughly delineated above in group c). There will be some pupils of overseas origin who will be speakers of a Great Britain based dialect of English, which is entirely uninfluenced by features deriving from an overseas dialect or language. These should be allocated to section A. We said as much in the introductory notes to that section. Remember, if you have doubts, allocate the pupil here, in section B. The more detailed questions which follow in the section should enable you to clarify the nature of the pupil's speech more exactly.

Note 2: How the section is organised
The section is in three parts, as follows:
Part B.1:   *Overseas dialect or language other than English?*
                    Also, which dialect? Which language?
Part B.2:   *How fluent and independent is the pupil as a reader*
                    and writer?
Part B.3:   *Does the pupil speak, in addition, any (or any*
                    further) language other than English or any (or any
                    further) overseas dialect of English?
We have separated the parts for convenience of filling in. Each
of these parts, however, contains no more than two or three
questions.

Note 3: Choice of overseas dialect or language other than
English (Part B.1)
This will be the next choice, after you have decided whether to
allocate the pupil to section B or section A. The issue will be
straightforward, we hope, for most pupils.
    A word about two complications.

(1)   We recognise that some pupils will be speakers both of
an overseas dialect of English and of a language other
than English. For example:
— a speaker of Grenadan standard who also speaks
Spanish;
— a speaker of London Jamaican who also speaks (e.g.)
a St. Lucian French Creole;
— a speaker of an African Standard who also speaks one
or more of the African languages.
And there will be others. Please try to decide here whether the
pupil's speech is predominantly an overseas dialect of English or
whether it is more accurately represented as heavily influenced
by a language other than English. We ask you to use your judgement and to allocate accordingly.

(2)   Similar considerations apply to pupils who speak more
than one language other than English. In this and in the
previous case we ask you to answer questions on the
basis of what you judge or ascertain to be the pupil's
dominant language. Reserve to the supplementary
questions in part 3, or to an explanatory comment,

any information about further languages or dialects.

Note 4: Overseas dialect of English (Sub-section B.1.1)
In the first part of the sub-section for speakers of an overseas dialect of English, we are concerned with the question: Which overseas dialect?
We realise this question is difficult. Specification of dialect across the shifting continuum of speech is difficult anyway. *For pupils of West Indian origin,* in particular, these general difficulties are compounded by two further factors:

(a)   the specific complexity of the dialectal situation in the Caribbean; and
(b)   added to this, the independent development and special status of some West Indian dialects (e.g. Jamaican creole) in Great Britain.

Don't worry, then, if your answer is based on a relatively rough and ready judgement.

In the question itself we try to help by offering *six very broad possibilities.* Let us try to explain these. Many pupils, we expect, may be straightforwardly assigned as *London Jamaican (a),* leaving till later questions the task of assigning the strength of the dialectal features and the extent of the pupil's use of the dialect. Others, though, (probably though not necessarily those who are recent arrivals in Great Britain) may speak *a version of Jamaican Creole (b) which is nearer to the original* or *another English based Creole (c),* which originates in another region of the Caribbean. Some will reflect an influence which is much closer to a *Caribbean, West Indian Standard (d).* Finally, there will be pupils, of other than Caribbean origin, whose speech reflects the standard (e) or differentiated, regional dialect (f) of another country (Africa, Australia etc.).

It may help to set out these central choices diagrammatically. The number beside each option relates to the corresponding possibility in question.

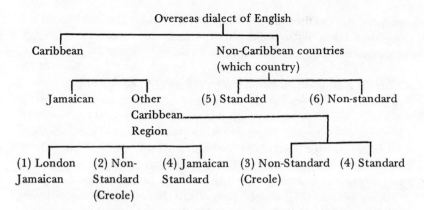

Most of us cannot make this kind of discrimination but rely on other sources of information. Use whatever help you can. For West Indian pupils specifically, if you still cannot discriminate, use the loose category of 'Caribbean'; and add any further information or comment you can.

Note 5: Strength of dialectal features (Q.17)
This is a further question in the sub-section concerned with speakers of an overseas dialect of English. Our focus in the question is on the strength of the *overseas* dialectal features in the pupil's speech. As we have said in connection with a similar question in section A, we are asking for a rough judgement only, based on an impression which will be the product of several, interwoven features. We have itemised some of these, such as idioms (turns of phrase), accent, intonation (patterns in the speech's rise and fall), syntax (grammatical constructions), style. But they are often not heard as distinct, separate features. We are asking for a judgement formed on your impressions.

Note 6: Language other than English (Sub-section B.1.2)
In the first part of the sub-section concerned with speakers of a language other than English, we are concerned with the question: Which language?
Clearly your best source of information about this will be the pupil. However, you should also have access to a language list, sent with this questionnaire, which should help form an impression of the most likely possibilities. Where in doubt, or where the situation is complex, please add an explanatory

comment. Further difficulties arising from the questionnaire in connection with speakers of a language other than English are, we hope, covered in what follows.

Note 7: Bilingualism and bidialectalism (Q.18, Q.21)
A further concern of ours, in both sub-sections of Part 1, is with the extent of the pupil's use of his overseas dialect or language. To repeat from our notes on Section A, specialisation of language for particular contexts is the usual form of bilingualism (and bi-dialectalism) to take. So the fact that a pupil may use a language other than English only for (e.g.) talking to his/her parents would not be a reason for denying bilingual status. We expect, then, that a number of pupils allocated to section B may be assigned as effectively bilingual or bi-dialectal. But by no means all. For some others the overseas dialect or language will be effectively the pupil's dominant language — the recently arrived English as a second language speaker, for example, or the recent arrival from Africa or the Caribbean. For others again, probably a rather greater number, the dialect or language will be essentially subordinate, either only partially known or relatively slightly used. Again, please add an explanatory comment if in doubt.

Note 8: Reading and writing (Part B.2)
The reading and writing of pupils allocated to section B is approached in two ways. *In part 1,* in the appropriate sub-section, *we ask about the reading and writing of the pupil in the overseas dialect or language.* We realise that in this, as in other questions in this part, you will have to rely heavily on your judgement of the pupil and on information which you gather from him/her.

In part 2, as in the corresponding part of section A, we also ask you to *make a rough estimate of the pupil's competence as a reader and writer.* The same considerations apply, as in section A. We are looking for your best rough estimate only. If none of the three possibilities fits, please feel free to add your own comment.

Note 9: Further languages or dialects (Part B.3)
In the third formal part of the section, we are interested *in any or any further languages or dialects* which the pupil may speak.
This will apply to some pupils only and is anyway supple-

mentary information to that which you will already have given. As we said in note 2 above, however, it is probable that some speakers of an overseas dialect of English in your class will also be speakers of a language other than English (a speaker of Grenadan standard (e.g.) who also speaks Spanish). Similarly some speakers of a language other then English may also speak an overseas dialect of English or, in some cases, a further language other than English. This linguistic richness is not always recognised as a feature of the language situation in the inner city. We should be grateful for any information you can offer about it.

Note 10: Part B.4
This will be self-explanatory. We'd be very grateful for anything you can offer — or your pupil, if you think it appropriate.

APPENDIX:
MOST COMMON LANGUAGES OTHER THAN ENGLISH

Afrikaans
Arabic
Bengali
Cantonese
French
Gaelic
German
Greek
Gujerati
Hakka
Hausa
Hindi
Ibo
Italian
Japanese
Malayan
Maltese

New Standard Chinese
Persian
Polish
Portuguese
Pushtu
Punjabi
Sinhalese
Serbo-Croat
Spanish
Swahili
Tagalog
Tamil
Twi
Turkish
Urdu
Yoruba

Appendix 2

UNIVERSITY OF LONDON
INSTITUTE OF EDUCATION
DEPARTMENT OF TEACHING OF
ENGLISH

SURVEY OF LINGUISTIC DIVERSITY IN ILEA SECONDARY SCHOOLS

Questionnaire

Research Director: Harold Rosen
Research Officer: Tony Burgess
Research Secretary: Antoinette Pernetta
English Dept., Institute of Education
20, Bedford Way, London WC1
(tel. 01-636 1500)

SURVEY OF LINGUISTIC DIVERSITY IN ILEA SECONDARY SCHOOLS

Detailed guidance in making the choices entailed in the questions which follow is contained in an accompanying booklet. We suggest that you read this first and keep it by you to refer to in any places where you are doubtful about how to answer for any particular pupil.

Further doubts can be resolved when we visit. We explain the nature of these visits in the booklet.

The questions which follow should be answered for one pupil only.

Filling in the questionnaire: instructions

(1) Please enter first the details of 'general pupil information' on the page immediately following these instructions (page 2).

(2) Then complete EITHER Section A OR Section B. Consult the accompanying booklet for guidance as to which section is applicable to this pupil.

(3) We ask you to complete all four parts of either Section A or Section B.

(4) Where there are sub-sections, complete only those which are applicable to this pupil. Omit other sub-sections.

QUESTIONNAIRE INFORMATION

NAME OF SCHOOL

TEACHER'S NAME(S)

DATE OF COMPLETION OF QUESTIONNAIRE

PUPIL CODE-NUMBER

PUPIL'S AGE ......years .....months

PUPIL'S SEX

164

SECTION A: A GREAT BRITAIN BASED DIALECT OF ENGLISH

PART A.1: WHICH DIALECT?
Please complete the questions in only one of the sub-sections in part 1.

EITHER: A.1.1 London
OR
A.1.2 Non-London
OR
A.1.3 Standard English

Choose the sub-section appropriate to the speech of the pupil.

Subsection A.1.1 London dialect of English
The pupil speaks a London, non-standard dialect of English not influenced by features which derive from other dialects or languages or from inexperience with English constructions and idioms.

Q1   HOW WOULD YOU ESTIMATE THE STRENGTH OF THE DIALECTAL FEATURES IN THE PUPIL'S SPEECH?
(Please select the most appropriate of the following possibilities and circle the number beside it)

- A full London: distinctive idioms, features of accent, intonation, syntax, speech style are all incorporated 1
- Mostly accent only   2
- Not accurately described by any of the possibilities above – (Please elaborate by adding a comment).   3

Subsection A.1.2 Non-London, Great Britain based dialect of English?
The pupil speaks a non-standard, Great Britain based

dialect of English which is spoken in a region (including Scotland, Ireland, Wales) outside London. Please also include in this section any London or Standard speaker, whose speech is influenced by a Great Britain based dialect, even if such influence is slight.

Q2 WHICH NON-LONDON DIALECT OF ENGLISH? . . . .

Q3 HOW WOULD YOU ESTIMATE THE STRENGTH OF THE DIALECTAL FEATURES IN THE PUPIL'S SPEECH?
(Please select the most appropriate of the following possibilities and circle the number beside it)

— A full dialectal speech of the particular region: distinctive idioms, features of accent, intonation, syntax, speech style are all incorporated.   1
— Mostly accent only, but the speech is not classsifiable as London or Standard.   2
— Basically London, but incorporating some features which derive from the non-London dialect of English. 3
— Basically Standard, but incorporating some features which derive from the non-London dialect of English. 4
— Not accurately described by any of the possibilities above — (Please elaborate by adding a comment).   5

Subsection A.1.3 Standard English
The pupil speaks the Great Britain based dialect known as Standard English. Please also include in this section any pupil whose speech is basically standard, but yet shows signs of convergence on (e.g.) London English. Do NOT include in this section pupils who speak an overseas based standard English (e.g. speakers of American Standard, Trinidadian Standard etc.)

Q4 HOW WOULD YOU ESTIMATE THE STRENGTH OF THE STANDARD ENGLISH FEATURES IN THE PUPIL'S SPEECH?
(Please select the most appropriate of the following possibilities and circle the number beside it)

— A 'full' Standard.   1

- Standard but with signs of convergence on London English. 2
- Not accurately described by either of the possibilities above — (Please elaborate by adding a comment). 3

PART A.2: READING AND WRITING
Please complete all questions in this part.

Q5 HOW WOULD YOU ESTIMATE THE PUPIL'S COMPETENCE AS A *READER* OF STANDARD ENGLISH?
(Please select the most appropriate of the following possibilities and circle the number beside it)

- Fluent and effective reader of English at a level appropriate to his/her age group; can manage most sorts of material without specific help. 1
- Intermediate: capable, but still 'inexperienced' as a reader, can not manage some kinds of material without help. 2
- Definitely has considerable difficulty. 3

Q6 HOW WOULD YOU ESTIMATE THE PUPIL'S COMPETENCE AS A *WRITER* OF STANDARD ENGLISH?
(Please select the most appropriate of the following possibilities and circle the number beside it)

- Fluent and effective writer of standard English at a level appropriate to his/her age group; rarely inconsistent with standard English constructions. 1
- Intermediate: capable, but incorporates dialectal features or reflects the normal signs of 'inexperience' as a writer in (e.g.) quality of construction, fullness of treatment, differentiation of style etc. 2
- Definitely has considerable difficulty. 3

Q7 PLEASE ADD HERE ANY FURTHER COMMENTS WHICH YOU MAY WISH TO MAKE ABOUT THE PUPIL'S READING AND WRITING.

PART A.3: FURTHER LANGUAGES AND DIALECTS
If appropriate, please complete the questions in both subsections in Part 3

167

A.3.1 A language other than English
AND
A.3.2 An overseas dialect of English

If the questions in either or both subsections do not apply to this pupil (i.e. he/she has the use of NO language other than English or NO overseas dialect of English), simply omit the subsections.

Subsection A.3.1

Q8 DOES THE PUPIL ALSO HAVE THE USE OF A LANGUAGE OTHER THAN ENGLISH?
(i.e. spoken in the family or by near relatives and friends)

— YES   1
— NO   2
(If YES, please answer Q9—Q10
If NO, please continue to Q12)

Q9 WHICH LANGUAGE? . . . .
(see accompanying languages list)

Q10 HOW EXTENSIVE IS THE PUPIL'S USE OF THE LANGUAGE OTHER THAN ENGLISH?
(Please select the most appropriate of the following possibilities and circle the number beside it)

— The pupil is effectively bi-lingual and speaks the language other than English regularly in certain contexts.   1
— The language other than English is the pupil's dominant language.   2
— The pupil has quite a good understanding of this language, but does not speak more than a few words and familiar phrases.   3
— The pupil hears this language in the family but does not speak more than a few words and familiar phrases. 4
— Not accurately described by any of the above — (Please elaborate by adding a comment).   5

Q11 DOES THE PUPIL READ AND WRITE IN THIS
LANGUAGE OTHER THAN ENGLISH?

—	READING	YES	1	1
		NO	2	2
—	WRITING	YES	3	3
		NO	4	4

Subsection A.3.2

Q12 DOES THE PUPIL ALSO HAVE THE USE OF AN
OVERSEAS BASED DIALECT OF ENGLISH?

—	YES	1	1
—	NO	2	2

(If YES, please answer Q13—Q15
If NO, omit further questions for this pupil)

Q13 WHICH OVERSEAS BASED DIALECT OF ENGLISH?...
(see Note 4, Introductory notes to Section B, page 10)

Q14 HOW EXTENSIVE IS THE PUPIL'S USE OF THIS
OVERSEAS BASED DIALECT OF ENGLISH?
(Please select the most appropriate of the following
possibilities and circle the number beside it)

— The pupil is effectively bi-dialectal and speaks the
overseas based dialect of English regularly in certain
contexts.   1
— The overseas based dialect is the pupil's dominant
dialect.   2
— The pupil does no more than occasionally adopt
some words, features of intonation, accent (etc.)
for certain effects or in some contexts.   3
— Not accurately described by any of the above —
(Please elaborate by adding a comment).   4

Q15 DOES THE PUPIL WELCOME THE OPPORTUNITY TO
READ OR WRITE SOMETIMES IN THIS OVERSEAS
BASED DIALECT OF ENGLISH, OUT OF INTEREST
IN IT?

(Please select the most appropriate of the following possibilities and circle the number beside it).

— Significantly interested in doing so   1
— Not particularly interested in doing so   2
— Opportunity is not realistically available within pupil's particular dialect   3
— Not accurately described by any of the above — (Please elaborate by adding a comment).   4

PART A.4 (OPTIONAL) ADDITIONAL COMMENTS

Please add here any additional comments which you would like to make. Alternatively you may like to ask the pupil to make a comment. Perhaps the following phrasing of our interest may help.

— *To teacher:* Can you add any other information which is relevant, including any languages spoken earlier in the pupil's life?
— *To pupil:* How do you think your language has changed over the last three years? We should be grateful for anything which you may like to tell us about this.

(End of Section A)

SECTION B: OVERSEAS DIALECTS OF ENGLISH OR LANGUAGES OTHER THAN ENGLISH?

PART B.1: WHICH OVERSEAS DIALECT OR LANGUAGE OTHER THAN ENGLISH
Please complete the questions in only one of the subsections in part 1

EITHER: B.1.1   Overseas dialects of English
   OR
   B.1   Languages other than English

Choose the subsection appropriate to the speech of this pupil.

Subsection B.1.1 Overseas based dialects of English
The pupil speaks an overseas based dialect of English or a Great Britain based dialect of English which is influenced by it. Please beware. Do not include in this section speakers of an overseas based dialect of a language other than English (e.g. French Creole).

Q16   WHICH OVERSEAS DIALECT OF ENGLISH?
(Please select the most appropriate of the following possibilities and circle the number beside it.
See Note 4, Introductory notes to Section B, page 10—11).

— London Jamaican   1
— Jamaican Creole   2
— Other Caribbean creole (English)   3
   (please also say which)
— A Caribbean Standard (English)   4
   (please also say which)
— English Standard of a non-Caribbean country
   (e.g. Africa, Australia, America etc.).   5
   (please also say which)
— Regional dialect (patois etc.) of a non-Caribbean

171

country (e.g. in Africa, Australia, America etc.) 6
(please also say which)
— Caribbean — loose categorisation only 7
— London/other Caribbean creole (English) 8
(please also say which)

Q17 HOW WOULD YOU ESTIMATE THE STRENGTH OF THE (OVERSEAS) DIALECTAL FEATURES IN THE PUPIL'S SPEECH?
(Please select the most appropriate of the following possibilities and circle the number beside it)

— A full dialectal speech of the particular overseas region, distinctive idioms, features of accent, intonation, syntax, speech style are all incorporated. 1
— Basically a London (or Standard) speaker, but incorporating some features (accent, intonation, some idioms), which derive from the overseas dialect of English. 3
— Not accurately described by either of the possibilities above — (Please elaborate by adding a comment) 3

Q18 HOW EXTENSIVE IS THE PUPIL'S USE OF THIS OVERSEAS DIALECT?
(Please select the most appropriate of the following possibilities and circle the number beside it)

— The pupil is effectively bi-dialectal and speaks the overseas dialect regularly in certain contexts. 1
— The overseas dialect is the pupil's dominant dialect. 2
— Basically a London (or Standard) speaker, but occasionally deepens the overseas dialectal features in certain contexts or for certain effects. 3
— Not accurately described by any of the possibilities above — (Please elaborate by adding comment). 4

Q19 DOES THE PUPIL WELCOME THE OPPORTUNITY TO READ OR WRITE SOMETIMES IN THIS OVERSEAS BASED DIALECT OF ENGLISH, OUT OF INTEREST IN IT?
(Please select the most appropriate of the following possibilities and circle the number beside it)

172

- Significantly interested in doing so   1
- Not particularly interested in doing so   2
- Opportunity is not realistically available within pupil's dialect   3
- Not accurately described by any of the above — (Please elaborate by adding a comment).   4

Subsection B.1.2 Languages other than English

The pupil speaks a Great Britain based dialect of English, but incorporates features which derive from a language other than English or which derive from inexperience with English constructions. Please also include in this section pupils who are learning English as a second language (at any stage); and pupils whose speech is influenced by an overseas dialect of a language other than English (e.g. French Creole).

Q20   WHICH LANGUAGE OTHER THAN ENGLISH? . . . . . .
(see accompanying languages list)

Q21   HOW EXTENSIVE IS THE PUPIL'S USE OF THIS LANGUAGE?
(Please select the most appropriate of the following possibilities and circle the number beside it)

- The pupil is effectively bi-lingual and speaks the language other than English regularly in certain contexts.   1
- The language other than English is the pupil's dominant language.   2
- The pupil has quite a good understanding of this language, but does not speak more than a few words and familiar phrases.   3
- The pupil hears this language in the family but does not speak more than a few words and familiar phrases. 4
- Not accurately described by any of the possibilities above — (Please elaborate by adding a comment).   5

Q22   DOES THE PUPIL READ OR WRITE IN THIS LANGUAGE? . . . .
(If YES, please indicate your estimate of the extent by circling one of the following alternatives)

173

- Reads capably and regularly in this language   1
- Reads only a little in this language   2

Q23 HOW WOULD YOU ESTIMATE THE PUPIL'S COMPETENCE AS A SPEAKER OF A BRITAIN BASED DIALECT OF ENGLISH (LONDON, STANDARD)?
(Please select the most appropriate of the following possibilities and circle the number beside it)

- Definitely in the initial stages of becoming a speaker of English.   1
- Intermediate: relates confidently to others in English, but is still significantly affected by inexperience with certain constructions and idioms.   2
- Fluent and effective speaker of English (though not necessarily Standard).   3

PART B.2: READING AND WRITING

Q24 HOW WOULD YOU ESTIMATE THE PUPIL'S COMPETENCE AS A READER OF STANDARD ENGLISH?
(Please select the most appropriate of the following possibilities and circle the number beside it)

- Fluent and effective reader of English at a level appropriate to his/her age group, capable of mastering most sorts of material without specific help.   1
- Intermediate: capable, but still affected by general inexperience as a reader or by inexperience with certain English constructions: unable to manage some kinds of material without help.   2
- Definitely has considerable difficulty.   3

Q25 HOW WOULD YOU ESTIMATE THE PUPIL'S COMPETENCE AS A WRITER OF STANDARD ENGLISH?
(Please select the most appropriate of the following possibilities and circle the number beside it)

- Fluent and effective writer at a level appropriate to his age group, rarely inconsistent with standard English constructions and idioms.   1
- Intermediate: capable, but still affected either by

174

general inexperience as a writer or by inexperience
with certain English constructions.   2
— Definitely has considerable difficulty.   3

Q26 PLEASE ADD ANY FURTHER COMMENTS WHICH
     YOU MAY WISH TO MAKE ABOUT THE PUPIL'S
     READING AND WRITING.

PART B.3: FURTHER LANGUAGES AND DIALECTS
If appropriate, please complete the questions in both sub-
sections in Part 3

        B.3.1 A language other than English
        AND
        B.3.2 An overseas dialect of English

If the questions in either or both subsections do not apply to
this pupil (i.e. he/she has the use of NO language other than
English or NO overseas dialect of English), simply omit the
subsections.

Subsection B.3.1

Q27 DOES THE PUPIL ALSO HAVE THE USE OF ANY
     (OR ANY FURTHER) LANGUAGE OTHER THAN
     ENGLISH?

        — YES
        — NO
     (If YES, please answer questions Q28–Q30
     If NO, please continue to question Q31)

Q28 WHICH LANGUAGE? ....
     (see accompanying language list)

Q29 HOW EXTENSIVE IS THE PUPIL'S USE OF THE
     LANGUAGE OTHER THAN ENGLISH?
     (Please select the most appropriate of the following
      possibilities and circle the number beside it)

        — The pupil is effectively bi-lingual and speaks the
          language other than English regularly in certain
          contexts.   1

175

- The language other than English is the pupil's dominant language. 2
- The pupil has quite a good understanding of the language, but does not speak more than a few words and familiar phrases. 3
- The pupil hears this language in the family but does not speak more than a few words and familiar phrases. 4
- Not accurately described by any of the possibilities above — (Please elaborate by adding a comment). 5

Q30 DOES THE PUPIL READ AND WRITE IN THIS LANGUAGE OTHER THAN ENGLISH?

— READING	YES	1	1
	NO	2	2
— WRITING	YES	3	3
	NO	4	4

Subsection B.3.2

Q31 DOES THE PUPIL ALSO HAVE THE USE OF AN OVERSEAS BASED DIALECT OF ENGLISH?

- YES 1 1
- NO 2 2

(If YES, please answer Q32—Q34
If NO, omit further questions for this pupil)

Q32 WHICH OVERSEAS BASED DIALECT OF ENGLISH?...
(see Note 4, Introductory notes to Section B, page 10)

Q33 HOW EXTENSIVE IS THE PUPIL'S USE OF THIS OVERSEAS BASED DIALECT OF ENGLISH?
(Please select the most appropriate of the following possibilities and circle the number beside it)

- The pupil is effectively bi-dialectal and speaks the overseas based dialect of English regularly in certain contexts. 1
- The overseas based dialect is the pupil's dominant dialect. 2
- The pupil does no more than occasionally adopt some

176

words, features of intonation, accent (etc.) for certain effects or in certain contexts.   3
— Not accurately described by any of the above possibilitities — (Please elaborate by adding a comment). 4

Q34   DOES THE PUPIL WELCOME THE OPPORTUNITY TO READ OR WRITE SOMETIMES IN THIS OVERSEAS BASED DIALECT OF ENGLISH, OUT OF INTEREST IN IT?
(Please select the most appropriate of the following possibilities and circle the number beside it)

— Significantly interested in doing so   1
— Not particularly interested in doing so   2
— Opportunity is not realistically available within pupil's particular dialect   3
— Not accurately described by any of the above —   4
(Please elaborate by adding a comment).

PART B.4: ADDITIONAL COMMENTS
Please add here any additional comments which you would like to make. Alternatively you may like to ask the pupil to make a comment. Perhaps the following phrasing of our interest may help.

To teacher: Can you add any other information which is relevant including any languages spoken earlier in the pupil's life.
To pupil: How do you think your language has changed over the last three years? We should be grateful for anything which you may like to tell us about this.

Index

Index by Ann Edwards